PRA

Make Money, Live Wealthy

Wealth is within your reach and this is the ultimate resource you need to learn how to obtain it starting today."

- Michael Kawula, *Bestselling Author of Connect, Serial Entrepreneur, Founder of SelfEmployedKing.com*

"I started reading Make Money, Live Wealthy and realized that I highlighted nearly the whole damn thing. Great book!"

- Ryan M., *book reviewer*

"Austin Netzley has the unstoppable combination of great intelligence AND incredible emotional intelligence. His authentic desire to help as many people as possible, coupled with his tactical strategies shared through his platform, makes him an ideal guide to one's financial picture.

Whether young and just starting out or perhaps more seasoned, yet needing to reset the ol' money mindset, anyone can flourish after embracing and implementing the teachings of Austin. Without a doubt, he is my go-to source when referring clients who have money blocks."

- Amber Hurdle, *Business and Leadership Coach, AmberHurdle.com*

"Money is woven into every fabric of our lives. Your level of understanding wealth and your ability to implement what you know greatly impacts the course of your life. In *Make Money, Live Wealthy*, Austin Netzley gets to the heart of how to build a wealthy life. Learn and implement his *10 Steps to True Wealth*, and build the life of your dreams!

- Ryan Michler, *Financial Advisor & Founder of Wealth Anatomy*

Make Money, Live Wealthy

75 Successful Entrepreneurs Share the 10 Simple Steps to True Wealth

Austin Netzley

ONE Press Publishing

Chicago

ISBN-13:978-1502985309

ISBN-10:1502985306

Dedicated to the greatest family under the sun. Thank you so much for all of the love and support from day number one. From driving me from sport to sport, to taking each of my crazy ideas in stride, you all have been more than amazing. You make my life a breeze, and I cannot thank you enough.

Table of Contents

INTRODUCTION

At the age of 27, I retired.

I didn't come from money, win the lottery, or sell a start-up company. What I did do—and what you can do, too—was learn some fundamentals on how to build wealth and then implement those practices into my life. The result has been a lot of money, but more importantly, it has also been something much more valuable: true wealth.

In this book, I intend to share how you, too, can get the same results.

Although I built my wealth quickly, I started out far from rich. Fresh out of college, I had an engineering degree and a lot of ambition, but I was held back by $80,000 of debt and a middle-class mindset.

A few years into my career, I started to read and network religiously. With each connection I made and every chapter I read, a whole new world opened up to me—one that promised I could achieve anything and become as rich as I chose to be. My mindset and perspective changed day after day, and my level of confidence and knowledge quickly grew to new heights.

I not only learned what wealth *really* is, but I also learned how to obtain it. While still working for the corporation, I started to invest heavily in the stock market and eventually began my first side-business. I grew that income stream and built up a large fund, and at 27, I was able to retire to travel the world and do as I please.

The money is great, but the most valuable thing I gained is complete freedom. I went from being totally stressed out and my own worst enemy to having peace of mind, confidence, and happiness.

However, this book is not about me at all—it is for you. It was written to show how you can build massive wealth and create the life of your dreams.

To help share some of the secrets of wealth I was fortunate enough to learn, I started YoPro Wealth, a blog and online radio show (called a podcast) dedicated to teaching people around the world what true wealth is and how to obtain it.

For the podcast, I interviewed iconic investors, bestselling authors, super successful entrepreneurs, financial planners, and other experts from all different walks of life on the subjects of money and success. The guests shared their journeys—the good and the bad, the ups and the downs—and the evolution they went through on their way to wealth. Shortly after starting, I began to recognize commonalities between them. The details of their stories were different, but they had all taken the same sequential steps, one after the next.

This book is a compilation of those stories, failures, successes, and advice from a total of 75 experts. It breaks down the wisdom they shared into ten simple steps that led each of them to true wealth. If you take these steps, you will obtain wealth in your life as well.

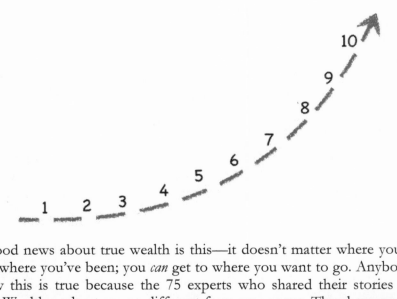

The good news about true wealth is this—it doesn't matter where you are in life or where you've been; you *can* get to where you want to go. Anybody can! I know this is true because the 75 experts who shared their stories on the YoPro Wealth podcast are no different from you or me. They have problems, challenges, mistakes, and flaws just like everyone else.

- It doesn't matter where you are in life.

Introduction

- o J. Massey started his real estate career while 'squatting' in a house he lost to the bank. He and his pregnant (and seriously ill) wife didn't have enough cash to eat for the next week, and J. himself had a punctured lung. Yet he started his new career and is now a sought-after real estate *investorpreneur*.

- It doesn't matter where you come from.

  - o "I'm a simple kid from Iran. I lived there during the revolution in 1989, and then I spent several years in a refugee camp in Germany." *-Patrick Bet-David, serial entrepreneur and author of Doing the Impossible*

- It doesn't matter how much money you have.

  - o David Wood went from being essentially broke to owning an island in just over a decade.

- It doesn't matter what your degree is.

  - o Ryan Holiday dropped out of college at 19 and became American Apparel's director of marketing at age 21.

- And it sure doesn't matter what your age is.

  - o Born into poverty, Trevor Blake didn't start his first business until he was in his 40s. Just a few short years later, he has sold multiple businesses for over $100 million each. To top it off, he added New York *Times* bestselling author to his list of accomplishments.

Each of the 75 experts have achieved these results by following a common process. Along the way, they have become rich, but they have also become *wealthy*—and that is much, much more important.

The Problem

Before we get started, let me ask you a question—*what is wealth?*

wealth – noun \'welth *also* 'weltth\
a large amount of money and possessions

By definition, wealth is all about money and possessions. However, if you ask people who are *actually* wealthy what their definition is, you get a completely different answer.

If we don't know what true wealth is, isn't it going to be hard to find it? Of course it is, and it shows up in the results.

The proof is evident. People want more in life—more happiness, more money, more freedom, more meaning. Studies show that 70% of people hate what they spend the majority of their life doing and are actively disengaged at work. America is #1 in depression, student debt and unemployment are strangling the younger generations, and the list goes on and on.

The problem starts with the way money, work, and wealth are depicted in society. True wealth is so much more than money and possessions, but we aren't taught this growing up. Most people assume that everyone understands wealth in the same way, but I've learned that this couldn't be further from the truth.

The rich are portrayed as superior—even evil. Those who are not rich, however, dream of being in the class where the challenges seem to be 'good problems' to have. So we continually chase money in pursuit of happiness, often putting this chase at the center of our lives.

We spend most of our time doing things we don't really want to do just because we get paid to do them. We've been trained to believe that work is painful. People say things like "Thank God it's Friday" and dread going to work on Mondays.

Retirement, a term created by a real estate developer in the 1960s, is represented as a period of joy where you can *finally* do what you want—but not until you're 65 (if you're lucky). We go through life just getting by, trying

Introduction

to make enough money to get to this point. But by then, we're at an age where we only have the energy, funds, and ambition to do so much. When we *finally* get to the goal, we realize with regret that there could have been more.

The good news is this: there *is* more. There is a life of wealth awaiting each and every individual. You just have to learn what the goal really is for you, and then how to obtain it. That is what this book is all about.

True Wealth

Figuring out the right destination is the first major hurdle that most people can't get past. We don't get in a car until we know our destination, yet most of us drive our lives without knowing where it is that we ultimately want to go.

Not only is true wealth not about money alone, it isn't a *thing* at all. It is a feeling, an idea, and a belief. It is many things wrapped up into one, and everyone will have their own version based on what is most important to them. Even so, when I asked most of the 75 experts to define wealth, common themes came up again and again.

To the wealthy, true wealth can be summed up in the following six categories.

Freedom

> True wealth is being able to do what I want, when I want. If I can do that, I am wealthy.
> —*JD Roth, Founder of GetRichSlowly.org, author of Your Money: The Missing Manual*

The strongest and most common word that came up in their definitions of wealth was *freedom*.

> Wealth is the freedom to choose. It is when your money works for you, and you have the choice to do what you want with your time and money.
> —*Steve Burns, author of the New Trader, Rich Trader series*

Freedom is the ultimate goal in life. This is what we're all after, and as a result, it's one of the greatest measures of success. The more freedom you have to do as you wish, the wealthier you are.

> I do not dismiss money because you need a certain level of wealth to create opportunities for your family. But wealth in the true sense is doing the things that you're passionate about, engaging with the people you want to engage with, and doing the things that are going to develop, improve, and enrich you.
> —*John Murphy, executive coach, founder of John Murphy International*

Experiences

> The wealthy value experiences, not things. Wealth isn't the accumulation of money; it is the accumulation of experiences. Wealth is not about your bank accounts. It has to do with how you use the money you're accumulating to live a rich life.
> —*Jason Vitug, CEO & co-founder of Phroogal*

The goal shouldn't be to *be rich* or *get rich*, but to *live rich*. There is an enormous difference. Living rich gives you a life full of experiences, excitement, and happiness.

> Wealth, to me, is holistic. It is the experiences that make me *feel* wealthy. Earn, save, and invest in a way that allows you to have the experiences you want to have.
> —*Kathleen Kingsbury, wealth psychology expert, author*

Happiness

> Wealth is happiness.
> —*Neil Patel, serial entrepreneur, founder of KISSmetrics*

Straightforward, but true—find complete happiness, and you are wealthy. The most common factor of happiness is the importance of relationships.

> We call ourselves 'famillionaires,' meaning we're rich beyond measure in our family. There are a lot of areas that define success and abundance in your life besides what you have in your bank account or what your

Introduction

financial portfolio looks like. True wealth for me means I have rich, loving relationships and vibrant physical health.
—Dan Miller, owner of 48 Days, LLC, bestselling author of 48 Days to the Work You Love

The key word in this quote is *abundance*. Most people view things from a scarcity perspective, but the wealthy see the world through the lens of abundance. This is a huge shift in your mindset that will make all of the difference in the world.

Wealth is an abundance of what you really want: family, money, physical health, the right mindset, and a healthy bank account.
—Mike Kawula, successful entrepreneur, founder of SelfEmployedKing.com

Fulfillment brings happiness. It's not how much of something you have, but how fulfilled you are by what you have. It's also about keeping the important areas of your life balanced in proportion to what you want.

Wealth is a well-balanced, happy life.
It is not about having a ton of money. It is about living richly—having a life rich in experiences, friendships, and relationships. It doesn't mean you don't have stuff; you have plenty of stuff. It just doesn't have *you*.
—Chris Locurto, speaker, leadership and business coach

Money

Lots of money can make you rich, but it doesn't necessarily make you wealthy. It is, however, a very important tool to help you get what you *really* want—freedom, peace of mind, etc.—because it does have a large impact on the other areas of your life.

Wealth is freedom and security.
—Mindy Crary, Certified Financial Planner (CFP), founder of Creative Money

Peace of mind is near the top of the list of the most priceless things in life. This is unfortunately a hurdle that most people never quite overcome. Take the financial advice in this book seriously so that you can escape your money worries once and for all.

Make Money, Live Wealthy

Wealth is being able to do the things you want without having to worry
about the money.
—Steve Stewart, debt expert, founder of Money Plan SOS

From a financial perspective, many experts have defined wealth as financial
freedom. Financial freedom is not a certain amount of money sitting in your
bank account—it is when your passive income (earnings made by doing
essentially no work) exceeds your expenses. This is the ultimate money goal,
and you will know all about it by the end of Chapter 8.

I'm focused more on financial freedom than on wealth: the ability to
live off your passive income, so you don't have to go to a 9-to-5 job
every day to generate the money you need to live.
—Rob Berger, attorney, founder of DoughRoller.net

Purpose

Purpose is wealth. Whatever you do, it has to come with a purpose.
—Larry Stevens, entrepreneur, founder of Opus Workspace

We all have a purpose, and to be our best, happiest, most successful selves,
we need to know what that purpose is and live in a way that supports it.

Wealth is being on your true north, where your passions, strengths, and
interests are meshed together. You must be on a path that nourishes
your soul. Otherwise, you won't stick to it. You also need to have a
strong number (financially) because it pays for the journey. But first and
foremost, you have to be on the right journey.
—JV Crum III, bestselling author of Conscious Millionaire

If you're on your True North, you live with passion and purpose. You're
doing what you were made to do and are probably great at it. If you're great at
something, the odds are that you can get a large monetary reward for doing it.
So being on your True North is one of the secrets of how the wealthy get the
'numbers to pay for the journey.'

Introduction

State of Mind

Wealth is a state of consciousness. It's about *thinking* wealthy and using that mentality to see wealth in your everyday life.
—*Brittney Castro, Certified Financial Planner, founder of Financially Wise Women*

Wealth is a state of mind—a belief. It is a constant balance of freedom, finances, experiences, relationships, happiness, purpose, growth, and contribution. It is a journey that never ends.

I don't equate wealth with a dollar amount; I look at money as part of a much bigger picture. Wealth is a state of being, a state of happiness, a state of success.

In order to achieve true wealth, you need a certain amount of money, but you also have to be living a life that is authentic and meaningful to you. You have to be constantly setting goals, going after things, driving yourself.

As long as you're on that journey, you're on your way to true wealth. And once you've tasted what it's like to be on that journey, whatever that is, you'll never want it to end.
—*Josh Brown, entrepreneur, franchise attorney, and founder of The Law Office of Josh F. Brown*

True Wealth:
Peace of mind | ABUNDANCE
FREEDOM
LIFESTYLE | *Experiences*
MONEY PASSION
Purpose | DIRECTION
HAPPINESS
HEALTH | *Relationships*
A State of Mind
GROWTH | *Contribution* | IMPACT
MAKE MONEY, LIVE WEALTHY

Why You Should Read This Book

The wealthy not only view wealth in a different way, but they also know how to obtain it in a completely different—and better and quicker—manner than everyone else. People say 'time is money,' but I believe the opposite to be even truer. *Money is time!* The more money you have, the more time you have . . . and time is the most valuable asset in the world.

You're reading this book because you want to become wealthy. In order to do so, there is only one prerequisite. It has nothing to do with where you come from, what education you have, or how rich your family is. The only requirement is that you take control of your past, your present, and—most of all—your future.

Most people never become wealthy because they simply skip this step. It's challenging, but becoming truly wealthy is not a get-rich-quick scheme. It takes time and is more of an internal journey than one of achieving financial success (although you'll become filthy rich in the process if you do it right).

Introduction

The wealthy often start out just like everyone else—if not worse—but at some point in time, they take control of their future and never look back. By reading this book, you are doing the exact same thing.

It is critical to go through each of the ten steps explained in this book. Some of the steps are not directly related to money, so you may find yourself wanting to jump ahead to the *exciting* parts (investing, entrepreneurship, Money Secrets of the Rich), but don't. Each and every guest will tell you to focus on the foundational pieces because that is what eventually creates massive success. Although you won't *feel* the results of some of these steps right away, they are absolutely necessary to make whatever you create last and grow.

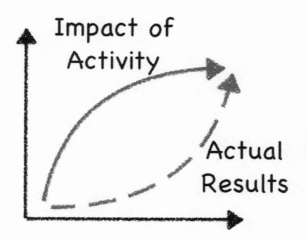

Why does it matter? Because . . .

- Money without happiness is not wealth.

- Riches without a strong foundation is a sure path to going broke (i.e. lottery winners).

- Entrepreneurship without awareness and clarity is nearly impossible.

- Success without the proper mindset is not sustainable.

If you do walk through these steps, here are five things that you will gain.

Direction

Most people think they lack money, but what they really lack is direction. My goal is to help you achieve clarity and direction in your life and, ultimately, get on your path to wealth.

A Plan

Achieving wealth is a complex thing. Where do you start? What do you do?

Let this book be your roadmap. You'll have a plan for getting to the next level in your personal life, your career, and your finances. You'll gain awareness of what is holding you back, and you'll also have a plan of attack and a list of priorities on which to focus.

Action

Getting started is the hardest part. My plan for this book is to inspire you to take action and show you the exact steps you need to take.

To help you do that, I have a number of videos and resources that will walk you through each chapter. To get these free resources, go to MakeMoneyLiveWealthy.com/bookguide.

As you make your way through the book, you will be able to identify where you are in the process and move forward one step at a time. Once you get into motion, you'll never look back.

More Money

What is the result of having direction and a structured plan and then acting on those things? More money, more wealth, and more of the other positive results that we all seek.

In reality, money is only a piece of the equation, but a lack of money does make everything a lot more difficult. As a result, how to make and keep more money is a key component of this book.

Remember that the goal isn't to make a ton of money just for the sake of being rich. The goal is to rid yourself of worry over your finances, so that the other priorities in your life—spending time with those you love, working on things you're passionate about, traveling—can be moved up on your list. The experts' advice will help get you to this point.

Wealth

Anybody can accumulate massive wealth in his or her lifetime, but wealth itself is not a destination. This isn't about a certain dollar amount or a certain status you need to have. Wealth is internal—it's all about having the right state of mind and the right balance.

> Discover what it takes to become wealthy, and you are wealthy.
> —*Chris Locurto*

This book will teach you what it takes. From there, it is up to you. As David Wood said, "Wealth is a choice." The choice is yours.

CHAPTER 1: TAKE CONTROL

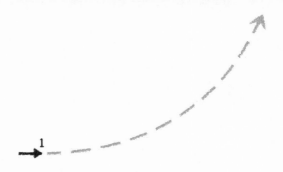

Make the Decision

The path to wealth starts with one thing: a decision.

Do you want to become wealthy?

Everyone says they do, but do you *really* want to become wealthy?

> Nothing starts until you make the decision and put in some sweat equity.
> —*Taylor White, international real estate expert*

When you truly make the decision, it becomes real. You fully commit and develop a belief that ensures that it is not a matter of *if* you will achieve your goals, but a matter of *when*.

David Wood spent ten years backpacking around the world, eventually ending up in Canada where he knew nobody. He had left school at fifteen, could barely read and write, and was completely broke. And yet he became a "multi-multi-multi millionaire" and created the life of his dreams. It all started when he made the decision.

> Realize you have a choice. Then make a decision and get into motion.
> —*David Wood, author, trainer, and business leader*

Chapter 1: Take Control

All success stories begin with a defining moment. Whether we're forced to make a decision, make it ourselves, or just get fed up with mediocrity and move toward freedom, this is the first step on your path toward wealth.

Passive income and online business expert Pat Flynn had his dream job working for an architecture firm. He was climbing the ladder, seemingly headed for success. Then the economy tanked in 2008, and Pat was let go from his job. Initially devastated, he went on to start some online businesses that now often bring in over $100,000 per month.

Entrepreneur and author Matt Shoup was also laid off from a corporate job. He had no choice but to commit to taking control of his future, as he had to bring in $3,000 in 22 days. So he started his first business and hasn't looked back since. He said, "That life event was a driving force for me early on."

Mike Michalowicz made his own decision that it was time for him to leave his company and create his future. Although he regretted it almost immediately at the time, it was the best decision he could have made.

> One day, exhausted from working so hard, I went out for drinks. With enough liquid courage in me, I said, "I'm going to start my own computer business." So I quit my job. I was 23, married with a child.
>
> The following day, hung over, I wanted my job back. My boss told me that not only was I not going to get my job back, but he would destroy my name, and no one would ever hire me.
>
> I went on but didn't know it was illegal to solicit clients from my old boss. He then sued me, but that was how I started.
> —*Mike Michalowicz, now a super-successful entrepreneur and bestselling author of The Toilet Paper Entrepreneur and Profit First*

Several other guests hit rock bottom and made the decision that enough was enough. From there, they quickly moved on to create the lives and income they desired.

> I had no idea what to do. I was depressed, spending a lot of money. On New Year's Eve in 2003, my frustration hit an all-time high. I promised

myself: 12 months later, I was not going to be in the same place. My life completely changed, once I made that decision.
—Patrick Bet-David

You won't get anywhere until you make that decision. Every single expert has done exactly that, and they haven't looked back. But you don't have to wait until you hit bottom or it's forced on you. John Lee Dumas and Dan Miller, among others, shared how they were doing well but saw an opportunity for more—and went after it. See the light and go! Make the decision *now* to live a wealthy life.

Successful people say, *Yes!* They make decisions. They know what they want to do, and they do it. They notice what is working and not working, and they're not afraid to adjust.
—David Wood

Control & Responsibility

Money is only a tool. It will take you wherever you want to go, but it will not replace you as the driver.
—Ayn Rand (shared by Brittney Castro)

Every successful person who appeared on my podcast had, at some point in time, stopped and realized that he or she wasn't living the life they wanted. At that point, they decided to do something about it. They took control and became the drivers in their own lives.

Financial and investment advisor Ryan Michler coaches his clients that the first thing they need to do—before figuring out which investments or insurances to buy—is to take control of their own financial destiny. Even though *he* will be managing their money, the clients are still the actual leaders of their financial lives.

Nobody cares more about your wealth and your money than you do, so you've got to own it. There are certain elements in life that you can't delegate: health, relationships, and wealth.

You have to know exactly what you're doing and why. You should work with financial advisors, accountants, and lawyers, but always keep

Chapter 1: Take Control

in mind: A great financial advisor helps you find the answers to your
own questions.
—Ryan Michler, Founder of Cittica Financial

You can delegate tasks, but the responsibility is still yours. As soon as you
realize that, you can make the major progress you're looking for.

Don't wait for permission to get to the next level. As soon as something
becomes a priority for you, you find a way to make it happen.

A big turning point for me was when I realized I was the creator. I was
the means, and money was just a tool.
—Mindy Crary

After studying human behavior and sports psychology for a few years, Coach
Mike Basevic started having personal challenges in his own life. His marriage
had ended and he was having business troubles, so he started asking himself
why these things were happening. He has since become a psychology and
performance expert, but before moving on, he had to take control of his own
life by taking responsibility.

During some research, I realized that most successful people—like Walt
Disney and Abraham Lincoln—failed at one time or another. They failed yet
moved along, and I can do the same exact thing.

So I stopped, accepted everything, and acknowledged: this is who I am,
and now I'm moving forward. These are the results I'm going to create.
I'm going to learn from my past, but I'm going to put that to one side,
get rid of all that baggage, and accept the fact that everyone has failures.
I'm going to concentrate on what I want to create in the future.
*—Coach Mike Basevic, behavioral strategist and performance coach, Founder of No
Limits Mental Edge*

You must take responsibility for your life as a whole, especially the important
aspects like your finances.

The bottom line is you can delegate *authority*, but you can never delegate *responsibility*. In the end, it's your money, and you're going to make your own decisions.
—Todd Tresidder, former investment hedge fund manager, current financial coach and author

Sometimes taking responsibility for mistakes or life events is much easier said than done, but you can only control what you can control. Accept things as they are and move onward toward where you want to go. Focus on improving.

As soon as you take responsibility for your life, you can change the world.
—Tom Basso, iconic investor spotlighted in Jack Schwager's Market Wizards series

Summary

A. The turning point is the moment when you decide to become wealthy.

The turning point for getting on the path toward wealth is making the decision and taking control of your life. Until you decide that enough is enough, you will never initiate change.

There are two types of people in the world: 1) people who sit back and go with the flow and 2) hungry people who will do whatever it takes to win. The hungry people choose results instead of excuses. They know they are the people who will be successful.
—Richard Wilson, founder of the Billionaire Family Office and other businesses under the Wilson Holding Company

B. Not making a decision is a decision in and of itself.

My best piece of advice is that nobody cares more about your money than you do. You need to take an active role in your financial life and your financial success.
—JD Roth

Chapter 1: Take Control

Don't say, "When I have the money, I will take it seriously." Take control of your finances once and for all so that money can come into—and stay in—your life. That's the first step.

C. You can delegate *authority*, but you cannot delegate *responsibility*.

When you truly make the decision to take responsibility for your past and future, the resources will show up in your life to help get you to your destination. You are the driver of your life, and you must steer it in the direction you want it to go. Nobody else is going to do that for you.

> This is your life—right now. What do you need to change in order to start toward where you want to be? The decisions you make will dictate which direction you take. Take responsibility. Don't blame somebody else.
> —*Tom Basso*

Action Items

1. This is your call to action. Are you going to continue as you have been, or are you going to do what you need to in order to achieve wealth? Will you commit to these 10 steps?

> The one essential action I'd recommend is: *decide*. Choose to make things different in your financial future. Get information. Use professionals. Take advantage of all the resources available to you. Get an education.
> —*Brittney Castro*

2. Get free videos and resources for this chapter at MakeMoneyLiveWealthy.com/chapter1.

3. Examine your past failures and think about the things that worry you today. Take responsibility, *let them go,* and move forward. You can't control everything that happens, but you can control the decisions you make. Whether the result is good or bad, it is nobody's fault but your own. Do not cast blame.

4. Take control of your future and the important areas of your life. Education, health, mindset, networking, relationships, money—these things are solely your responsibility.

> Take control of your own education. Stop putting off the books you want to read, the articles you want to absorb, the topics you need to study. Do them right now!
> *—Ryan Holiday, who dropped out of college at 19, but now reads at least an hour per day*

Step 1 Checklist:

Goal	Complete?
Make the decision and commit to becoming wealthy.	
Take responsibility for the past and move forward.	
Take control of your future.	

CHAPTER 2: DEVELOP A WEALTH MINDSET

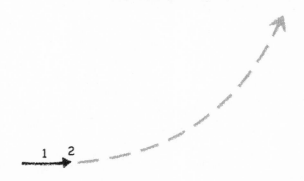

Mindset isn't an important thing. It is the only thing.
—*Mark Sieverkropp, author of Project: Success and co-host of Happen to Your Career podcast*

Wealth and success start and end with one thing—your mindset.

This is step 2 of the 10 steps to true wealth, but it is the most important of all. Mike Kawula said, "If you don't have the right mindset, you will never be wealthy." Why is this so critical?

Well, thoughts lead to feelings, which lead to actions, which lead to results. If you want better results, you have to start with the right thoughts.

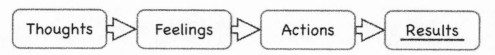

Being aware [of] and controlling your thoughts will take you far in life. Every action starts with a thought. Cultivate a mindset that's ripe for success.
—*Jason Vitug*

Whether you realize it or not, the environment in which you grew up programmed you a certain way. From our school system to our peers, from our parents to what we watched on television, our surroundings shaped our beliefs and our subconscious thoughts and values.

Unfortunately, many of these things are not supportive of wealth and success, and so we become our own greatest enemy.

Greatest Enemy

99.8% of all of our limitations are self-imposed.
—August Turak, successful entrepreneur and award-winning author of Business Secrets of the Trappist Monks

There is only one thing holding us back from achieving all the wealth and success that we want in the world—ourselves.

We spend so much time worrying and blaming, but nearly all of our limitations come from within! We hate when other people tell us we're not good enough or we're going to fail, yet this is how we talk to ourselves every single day without even realizing it!

It's the way we've been programmed through society and evolution. We've been taught to think that failure is bad, and therefore we must stay within the boundaries, listen to the rules, and follow the crowd. As kids, we were told we could be anything we wanted to be. Slowly but surely, however, we're taught to have more 'realistic' expectations, and we get funneled down the most commonly accepted path.

This programming starts early on, and it impacts us for the rest of our lives. Financial planner and mindfulness expert, Leisa Peterson, states that our money personality is set by the age of seven.

Very few people feed their children a wealthy mindset: that the universe is abundant, that we can have wealth and success, that we can be happy, and that it's okay to have nice things and live a comfortable lifestyle.

The majority of people are taught just the opposite. Whether it's through society, media, or whatever, we're raised in a fear-based environment. That's our conditioning. Our subconscious mind captures

Chapter 2: Develop a Wealth Mindset

all of those images and beliefs, and we start creating the same results in
our life that we were taught as a child.
—Coach Mike Basevic

When we start to get too far away from what is considered *normal* for us, anxiety, fear, and doubt set in and try to bring us back to our comfort zone. We don't *feel* like we are going to succeed (remember the formula—our feelings lead to our actions), so we stop ourselves from going any further.

Our quiet mind, our subconscious, rules 90-95% of our day. The
subconscious mind records images from the time we're born to the
time we die. We use our perception of these events to develop our own
beliefs, habits, and conditioning based on the visual images and our
perceptions. Then we play it back in our reality.
—Coach Mike Basevic

Our greatest fears are those of humiliation or embarrassment, so we try to avoid the possibility of those things at all costs. The way to do this is to keep doing only the things you know, but that doesn't get you to where you want to be.

Great improvements and massive successes only come from stepping outside your comfort zone. They happen when you reach, stretch, and become vulnerable. Develop a belief in yourself and you *will* get out of your own way.

My best piece of advice came from Dr. James Gills, the only man to
complete six double Ironmans (a 281.2 mile race). He completed his
last one at the age of 59. I asked him how he did it. He said, "It was
simple, really. I have learned to talk to myself instead of listen to myself.
If I listen to myself, I hear all the negative, all the fear, all the
complaints, and all the doubts. But if I talk to myself, I can feed myself
with the words and encouragement to keep on running, to keep on
moving forward.
—Jon Gordon, bestselling author of The Energy Bus, The Carpenter, and more

We are the only ones who hold ourselves back because we give our fears and doubts air time. Don't *listen* to yourself. *Talk* to yourself.

Reprogram Your Mind

Our beliefs are just thoughts with emotions tied to them that we've
taught ourselves to believe are true.
—JV Crum III

Our beliefs shape everything we do, but we have to realize that they aren't real. They are only figments of our imagination.

Beliefs are not based on experiences; they are based on interpretations
of experiences.
—Dr. Dennis Cummins, bestselling author and expert trainer

The most impactful thing you can do is change your mindset. This will have a domino effect in every area of your life. The good news is that it doesn't matter what your beliefs are—you can change them. The first step that several wealthy guests have suggested is to identify the specific beliefs that are holding you back—fittingly called *limiting beliefs*.

The most common limiting beliefs are always based around worthy and
deserve. You don't think you deserve or are worthy of something, and
that belief affects your wealth.
—JV Crum III

Changing your mindset is an absolutely critical part of the process. You must get real with yourself and identify those beliefs that are stopping you from achieving the level of success and wealth that you want. What major thoughts and emotions about money, success, and relationships are hindering you from becoming the person you want to be?

One of the best ways to find your limiting beliefs is to chronicle your thoughts and feelings about the key areas of your life in a journal. What beliefs cause fear, frustration, and stress to flare up? Our subconscious doesn't know time, so events that happened decades ago can be just as impactful as those that happened yesterday. Our core limiting beliefs often come from a time well before we reached the age of 18. As a result, revisiting your childhood is a key way to uncover the limitations affecting your life today.

Chapter 2: Develop a Wealth Mindset

As we grow up, we learn about money from watching other people and
from our own experiences. This creates our blueprint about how
money works and determines how we interact with money. Some of it
is correct, but some of it is incorrect.
—JD Roth

This blueprint essentially sets us up for a certain level of wealth and success.
It represents how we think and feel about things, and it predisposes us to
certain actions. If we stray too far from what is familiar—or too far from the
level of success we expect—we ultimately make decisions (unconsciously) that
bring us back. It works much like the thermostat in your house.

This is why so many poor people who win the lottery end up broke again in a
couple of years. On the other hand, you see people like Donald Trump, who
filed for bankruptcy only to be a massive success once again only a few short
years later. The truth is that you have a set level for success in other areas of
your life, too.

It's your financial blueprint, and it is every other blueprint that you've
got, too: relationships, diet, health. We all think and act in certain ways
based on our past conditioning and experiences.
—Dr. Dennis Cummins

Fortunately, you can control and change this seemingly preordained path by
taking the right steps. JV Crum III, who has a master's degree in clinical
psychology, shared his 7-step Rapid Belief Change Technique:

1. Acknowledge and write down what you're gaining from each belief. No
belief continues to exist unless you get something from it (feeling sorry for
yourself, getting to play the victim).

2. Write down what each belief is costing you.

3. What are some examples counter to this belief? These are public people
or people you know personally who are living lives opposite to this belief.

4. Create an empowering belief. Simply reverse your limiting belief.

5. Look for examples of people who live that empowering belief. When you do this, you access different parts of your brain. This is not the same as doing the opposite of your belief (from step 3).

6. Write down what you will gain from holding this new belief.

7. Get into action and start moving forward. What is one goal you'd like to achieve in the next 24 hours? What are three steps you can take to start moving in that direction?

Our subconscious doesn't recognize what is real and what is not. If you say something a number of times and add your emotions to it, you can trick your mind and reprogram it.

After being told that he would never walk again, Hal Elrod could have easily felt sorry for himself and given up. Instead, he created an unstoppable mindset. Not only did he walk again, but he soon ran an ultra-marathon. The key step that he took in building that mindset was creating an unstoppable mindset by using written affirmations.

> I discovered that affirmations are the most effective way to design my ideal mindset and program my mind for success. There's no limiting belief that you cannot replace with an empowering belief by putting it in writing, designing the program that you want for your subconscious mind, and programming it every single day.
> —*Hal Elrod, keynote speaker, coach, and bestselling author*

Hal mentioned a subtle, yet important, factor—*every single day*. You have to create the habit and continue to fuel that fire. Practice doesn't make perfect; it makes permanent.

> We are what we repeatedly do. Excellence is a habit. Wealth is a habit.
> —*August Turak*

Create the right practices and keep improving, and wealth will be yours. If you're having trouble creating the mindset and beliefs, start with what you *do* have.

Chapter 2: Develop a Wealth Mindset

If a thought or concern doesn't help get you where you want to go, dismiss it. The first part of stopping that inner demon is to become aware of it. The second part is to act in spite of it.

One of the key money beliefs that hold people back is, 'I'm not good with money.' None of us were born being good with money. We all have to learn to deal with money.

We all say, 'I'm not good enough, smart enough, pretty enough, innovative or creative enough.' Instead of tearing yourself down, learn how to celebrate what you do have to offer. Coming from a place of self-love is getting out of your own way.
– *Kate Northrup, author of Money: A Love Story*

By focusing on the positive, you see things in a completely different light—and it impacts everything else. This is one of the many uncommon secrets shared on the podcast. The way to turn things from negative to positive begins with gratitude. By doing so, you rewire your brain.

Dr. Dennis Cummins also talks about gratitude in his bestselling book, *Turning Terrible into Terrific*. Dennis shared the three steps he has found to turn any situation to terrific.

Step #1 is to start with gratitude. Be grateful for what you've got.

It's easy to be grateful for the things in your life when everything's going well. The challenge is to find something to be grateful for when they're really not going well, when things are really terrible. How do you look through all the junk, all the things that are not good, to find the one thing that is? If you start focusing on that, you start to develop a more positive attitude.

Step #2 - You've got to have focus. What is it that you *really* want?

People often take action based on their little wants, the things that aren't really important but are just short-term things that bring them short-term happiness. So what do you really want? What will make your life excellent? If you can crystalize that, then it's going to make things a lot easier.

The third step, and probably the most critical, is to take action. All the thinking, hoping, and coaching in the world isn't accomplishing anything unless you do something.

Action is often the most complicated because we human beings don't like to change. Our minds are set up to enjoy what is comfortable and familiar, so we resist change.

My suggestion is to do one small thing every day. People try to do too much, which causes fear, which in turn causes the brain to resist. Change makes us uncomfortable, but before long you'll be comfortable with being uncomfortable.

If you do just one small thing a day, the brain doesn't even realize you've done anything, so it stops being afraid. I call it a 'sneaky success.' You do one little thing at a time, and the change is so small that your brain doesn't even notice that you changed. But do a little bit each and every day for a whole year, and by the end of the year, you will have achieved dramatic change.
–Dr. Dennis Cummins

As Dennis says, "Put those three things together, and you can change anything in the world."

1. Have gratitude for where you are, no matter where that is.

2. Be really clear about where you want to go.

3. Just take one step toward that goal each and every day.

Think Rich

Rich people think big. Poor people think small. Rich people play the money game to win. Poor people don't want to lose, so they fear taking risks.
–Michael Kawula

If you want to be rich, you have to think like the rich do. You have to think big and develop an internal confidence about what you can achieve.

Chapter 2: Develop a Wealth Mindset

> If you don't have a lot of conviction in what you're doing, every book
> you read and every person you meet will distract you and get you off
> track.
> —*Richard Wilson*

It is essential to set the intention and create that belief in your mind. If you don't believe you can do something, who will? Making a sale, getting a raise, succeeding in your business—all of these things start with believing in yourself. If you truly believe in your ability, other people will believe in you as well. Your mind manifests what it creates.

You have to own your story, take responsibility for your past, and believe in your future. Justin Williams was $120,000 in debt, but he developed the mindset that he wasn't going to allow challenges to stop him—and he turned his business around.

> Those experiences made me who I am. Now, I believe that I can
> overcome any obstacle that stands in my way.
> —*Justin Williams, successful real estate investor and entrepreneur*

The wealthy use their temporary failures as lessons. They get better and stronger from each and every one, eventually learning that nothing can stand in the way of their success.

> It's never whether you can or can't; it's always whether you will or
> won't. If you believe you can, you will. If you believe you can't, you
> won't.
> —*Dr. Dennis Cummins's own version of the great Henry Ford quote*

One of many 'secrets' mentioned over and over by the experts is utilizing visualization and different forms of the law of attraction. You may roll your eyes, thinking this borders on the 'woo-woo' side, but it's worth taking very seriously.

> The principle of entrainment is incredibly powerful. If you have two
> oscillating systems and leave them in the presence of each other, after a
> while they will start to oscillate or cycle together. This principle was
> discovered by some scientists who had these giant grandfather clocks,
> with heavy pendulums, in the building where they had their lab. The

pendulums were swinging out of sequence, but over the course of several days they started to go left right left right together in cycle. They called this principle 'entrainment.'

Our thoughts are electrical energy that can be measured by an EEG. If you have a certain pattern of thought, you create a certain cycle of energy. Because of the law of entrainment, you attract like energies into that sphere, and they start to synchronize with you. That's why people say 'like attracts like.' That's why we enjoy and like people who are like us—because we already have that built-in synchronicity.
—Dr. Dennis Cummins

If you think in the right way, you'll attract opportunities into your life that will help you get what you want. It is then just a matter of what you do with those opportunities.

<u>Summary</u>

A. The mindset is everything.

Everything comes from within you. The mindset is where it starts.
—Anton Ivanov, self-made millionaire, money coach

Mindset is the most important thing to develop on your way to wealth. It doesn't matter whether it is your health, money, relationships, happiness, business, or anything else—it all starts with the beliefs and the attitudes you possess.

Smart money management is more about mindset than it is about math.
—JD Roth

B. We are our own worst enemy.

The two biggest hurdles that most people have are overcoming their personal internal battles and setting their mindset up to create the life of their dreams. Mark Sieverkropp states that this is 90% of the battle.

Chapter 2: Develop a Wealth Mindset

Just punch fear in the face, because it is only there as a safety
mechanism from back when we were cavemen.
—Pat Flynn

C. True wealth is a mindset and a belief, not a destination.

Once you develop the right mindset, you are only several actions and a little bit of time away from wealth. The truly wealthy know how to obtain it and have confidence in their ability to do so.

If I lost everything, I know how to get here again. Discover what it
takes to become wealthy, and you are wealthy.
—Chris Locurto

True wealth cannot be spent. It is a combination of having the right knowledge, beliefs, and level of fulfillment in your life.

Wealth is something that can't be taken away. I have a wealth of
knowledge, and that is where true power lies.
—John Dumas

D. To get new results, reprogram your mind first.

The reason the mindset is so important is because our thoughts ultimately create our results.

To change our results, we must change our initial beliefs. Life and our experiences have programmed us in a certain way, so to get to our peak level of success, we have to identify our limiting beliefs and reverse them. We must reprogram our mind for success and begin to think like the wealthy do.

Make Money, Live Wealthy

E. The rich think differently.

The rich think big. They have an internal confidence. They think in terms of abundance, not in terms of scarcity. Instead of holding themselves back, they become supporters for their own success.

> If I had to do it all over again, I would lean forward even more and listen less to people. I would have moved faster and more aggressively. I would have been more confident about the value I was adding to the world.
> —*Richard Wilson*

In addition, instead of sitting back and allowing things happen *to* them, they *make* things happen. They envision the results they want to achieve, and they manifest those things in their life—they start with beliefs and then make them real. Instead of *listening* to themselves, they *talk* to themselves.

We cannot control everything, but we are the masters of our own actions and reactions. Control and direct your thoughts, and the results will take care of themselves.

> Your mindset is the choice that you make. It's a straight line: mindset and results.
> —*John Murphy*

Changing the world starts with changing *your* world. The result is wealth—in all senses of the word.

	__Poor__	__Wealthy__
The Key to Becoming Wealthy	Luck	Having the right mindset

Action Items

Chapter 2: Develop a Wealth Mindset

1. Get the free resources for this chapter at MakeMoneyLiveWealthy.com/chapter2, including private videos and more.

2. Commit to creating a wealthy mindset. It is the most important thing you can do for your success. If you focus on just one thing, focus on this.

"The one action I'd suggest is to realize *you can change the world!* If you're going to change the world, whether or not you become financially wealthy, you're going to have the wealth that really matters, and that's inside. If you're going to change the world through a product or idea or information, wealth is going to naturally result. If you don't have that mindset, immediately shift to it." – *Matt McWilliams, author, Founder of Matt McWilliams Consulting, Inc.*

3. Identify any limiting beliefs. Journal the things that hold you back from becoming all that you can be.

4. Reverse those limiting beliefs by using JV Crum III's 7-Step Mind-Change technique.

5. Create new healthy mindset habits and repeat them on a daily basis. Affirmations, a vision board, and meditation are great places to start.

CHAPTER 3: CREATE THE ENVIRONMENT

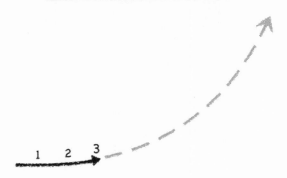

What you think about and who you hang out with . . . you become. As a result, if you want to reach new heights in your life, you must create the surroundings that will help get you there. This is the critical element #3 necessary for you to obtain true wealth.

Becoming and staying wealthy is not easy, especially if you attempt to do it on your own. To achieve everything you want to achieve in the quickest and easiest manner, you have to build and surround yourself with the proper environment—the right information, an expansive network, and a personal team that will help support and guide you to your destination. In doing this, you not only promote the right habits, but you also reprogram your mind for that next level of wealth.

Environment		
Information	Network	Team

The Right Information

Invest in yourself. When you do this, you press the fast forward button
on your success.
—*John Dumas*

Many experts have built a fortune through various investments, yet every single one of them will tell you that the best investment you can make is in yourself. There are several ways to do this, but the main way is through personal development via books, conferences, online training, podcasts, and similar mediums. These are important aspects of your success.

I love the quote from Jim Rohn, 'Learn to work harder on yourself than
you do on your job,' because if you work hard on your job, you might
be able to make a living; but if you work hard on yourself, you'll be able
to make a fortune.
—*Peter Voogd, serial entrepreneur, trainer*

What you feed your mind with not only creates how you think, but also determines how you act. It is your habits that create your success—or lack thereof—and investing in yourself is the #1 habit you can have.

The wealthy use their spare time to fill their heads with the right information. They are lifelong learners, always searching for new and different ways to expand their minds.

The most important asset we have is our mind. You should be spending
time expanding yourself in terms of knowledge and your peer group.
—*Ann Wilson, self-made millionaire and author of The Wealth Chef*

Hal Elrod was depressed, his business was struggling, and it was hard for him to think clearly. He searched Google, finding a quote by Jim Rohn that changed his whole life: "Your level of success will rarely exceed your level of personal development."

It occurred to Hal that he had not been dedicating time every day to his personal development or putting the right information in his mind. As a result, he was not becoming the person who could create the success he wanted.

Make Money, Live Wealthy

If you're measuring success on a scale of 1-10, we all want 10 in every area—health, happiness, finances, energy, relationships—but the distinction that I made is, if our level of personal development in any of those key areas is not at the level 10, then our level of success is going to parallel wherever our level of personal development is.

At that moment, I decided to take an hour each day at 5 a.m. for personal development. I realized that personal development was the gift I can give to myself every single day.

My depression was gone within 24 hours, and within two months of starting my morning routine, I had more than doubled my income. I ended up going from being in the worst shape of my life to training for the 52-mile ultra- marathon.
—Hal Elrod

Hal made personal development a priority in his life, and he got up an hour earlier to get it done every day. This routine of daily personal development changed his life so dramatically that he started calling it *The Miracle Morning*—now also the title of his bestselling book.

It's never about *having* the time—you have to *make* the time. You have to make personal development a top priority each and every day.

Carve out some time in your day. Stop whining that you don't have any time because you do. Stop being lazy in the morning; use that time to improve yourself.
—John Dumas

You have to take responsibility and control your education, just as you do with your money.

Having left college, I understood that education was my responsibility. No one was going to do it for me. If I wanted to get ahead and stay ahead, I would have to dedicate myself to directing my own education. I consider reading a book to be part of my job and spend a minimum of one hour a day reading.
—Ryan Holiday

Chapter 3: Create the Environment

Read books, listen to CDs or podcasts in the car or while at the gym, watch inspiring and educational videos—it doesn't matter what the medium is as long as it becomes a habit. Consider it part of your job.

> Before I turned 30 years old, I had already read 500 books on business, on relationships, on marriage, on finances, on many different subjects that I wanted to study. Those books became my mentors. Those books became my advisory board.
> *—Patrick Bet-David*

Does this seem excessive? Maybe, but that is what it takes some people to reprogram their mind for success as quickly as possible.

The year after Peter Voogd said 'enough is enough' and decided to pursue his true wealth, he studied every single book he could find on entrepreneurship, productivity, and wealth. The result was a 30% increase in sales even while working 15-25 hours less per week.

Do you see why investing in yourself is the best single investment you can make? With the right information and surroundings, you can quickly change your attitude and, more importantly, your results.

Network = Net Worth

> Your network: that is the #1 key to success.
> *—David Wood*

> You become the sum of the five people with whom you spend the most time. If you don't walk away from a conversation feeling bigger or more empowered, then you need to hang around with some new folks. That's the #1 mistake that young people make. They hang around with the wrong crowd for the wrong set of reasons, and they end up living a smaller life because the people they are around do not think big thoughts.
> *—David Wood*

Your environment creates who you become. If you want to be rich, talk to and hang out with rich people. If you want to be happy, surround yourself with people who are positive and happy. It's not rocket science. Plus, the people you associate yourself with can open the doors to so many opportunities.

> If you meet someone one who is important and successful, guess who they know and spend a lot of time with? It's other successful people.
> —*Ryan Holiday*

The beautiful thing about a strong network is that you don't have to know all the answers—you just have to be able to *find* the answers. With a solid and reliable network, someone can surely point you in the right direction, saving you a lot of time, effort, and money.

It's not only who you know that is a key differentiator, but also *who knows you*. Networking—just like personal development and self-education—should be considered a part of your job.

In short, the right network will take you where you want to go. Without it, it becomes considerably more difficult to become all that you can be.

> Being around people that are trying to push you towards those goals is such a necessary thing when you're trying to do something unconventional.
> —*Sean Ogle, entrepreneur and traveler, founder of Location 180*

Build Your Team

> Look at the people you admire. Spend time with them, pick their brains, and learn from them. Don't take financial advice from people not in the financial position where you want to be.
> —*Matt Shoup*

One of the most common mistakes shared by the experts was that most people take advice from people they wouldn't even trade places with. There is a lot of information out there, but so much of it is not very good. You have to learn who to trust and listen to.

> The best thing for me is, learn from those you aspire to be like, and ignore everyone else.
> —*Billy Murphy, serial entrepreneur, founder of Blue Fire Poker*

Chapter 3: Create the Environment

You should not only have a large network of contacts, but you should also have your own team of advisors. One of the most consistent commonalities among the wealthy is that they have mentors and coaches for the important areas of their life. The best of the best have a team guiding them to become even better.

> With a coach, you can cut your learning curve in half and get to your success quicker. People always say, 'Learn from your mistakes,' but in reality, that's a pretty expensive way to learn. If you learn from other people's mistakes, you'll cut your learning curve in half while saving a lot of aggravation, headache, stress, time, and money.
> *—Peter Voogd*

	Non-Wealthy	**Wealthy**
View Coaches As:	A cost.	An investment.
How to Achieve Their Goals:	By working harder, doing things themselves.	With the guidance of people who have already done what they want to do.

I asked many of the successful guests what they'd do starting out to help them get to a high level of success even quicker, and they had a very common answer—get a great mentor or coach ASAP!

> If I were doing it all over again, I would go right out and find a mentor instead of trying to figure it all by myself. I would have gone very, very quickly, found somebody in my space that's the best. I would have treated them, taken them out to lunch, sent them gifts—whatever I could to bribe them to be willing to mentor me and work with me.
> *—Patrick Bet-David*

August Turak shared the story of how he reached out to people he thought could teach him the most. He called Louis R. Mobley (founder of the IBM Executive School) to ask him if he would teach him everything he knows.

I reached out to someone I admired and respected, and I said, "I want to learn from you. I will find you clients if you teach me everything you know." I went there for life advice, not for business advice, but got the most unbelievable education of a lifetime.
—August Turak

People aren't born with the perfect network or knowledge. It is by taking action, reaching out to those you admire, and helping other people that you expand your network and ultimately create a team destined for success. When you do, wealth is right around the corner for you.

Summary

A. The best investment you can make is in yourself.

Since *you* are the best investment you can make, it's imperative to create surroundings that breed success. By doing so, you not only promote the right habits, but you also reprogram your mind for that next level of wealth.

The stuff you fill your head with is key.
—David Wood

Investing in yourself means any type of personal development—finding and utilizing anything that feeds your mind and allows you to grow as a person. Examples are self-education (books, podcasts, audio recordings), training, conferences, experiences, networking, and conferences. These are all things that can change your life.

B. You become who you hang out with.

You are the average of the five people you spend the most time with. Take a good look at who you're associating with.
—Mike Kawula

If you want to improve your life, improve your network. If you want to make more money, change your network so you're spending your time with successful people. Surround yourself with those whom you aspire to be like and ride the wave to success.

Chapter 3: Create the Environment

Not only do you become those five people, but your income will reflect the earnings of that group within 10-15%, per David Wood. So seriously consider your core network—it can bring you up or pull you down. The choice is yours.

C. Build your team.

When you depend on mentors who have been-there-done-that, you hit the fast-forward button. You don't waste time, energy, and effort.

When I first started, I went out and found a mentor. It wasn't cheap; it was an investment. I wasn't just paying for $1^1/_2$ hours every week, but I was engaging with her. I was paying for her years of knowledge, all of the connections and relationships she had built. To this day, I am still investing in myself.
—*John Dumas*

Every wealthy individual has a team of mentors and coaches for the important areas of his or her life—money, health, personal and business relationships. If you surround yourself with people who have already arrived at the place you want to be, they'll pull you upward.

There are endless possibilities when you have a mentor. You shift your circle of influences, share knowledge, and have more opportunities. It'll increase your income and influence, and it'll raise your profile, lower your stress, and raise your awareness. I surround myself with people who are already where I want to go.
—*Peter Voogd*

More people than you would expect are willing to help. It pays to be brave and savvy enough to reach out. Plus, a network is something that grows exponentially. One solid contact opens the doors to so many other people from whom you can benefit. Just build it one contact at a time, and the effects will be enormous.

The right network can keep you motivated and focused as you feed off the energy of those around you. They can help you get back on your feet in tough times and thrive in good times. It is a daunting challenge to do things on your own, so you shouldn't do so.

Action Items

1. Find and utilize the videos and resources for this chapter at MakeMoneyLiveWealthy.com/chapter3, including an exclusive offer to join our growing group of ambitious professionals looking to build true and massive wealth.

2. Find a way to reduce your expenses by 10-20% and use that money to invest in your education or network.

3. Create an environment that breeds success. If necessary, cut out the habits or people that are holding you back. This is one of the most important action steps that you can take—*period.*

"Start finding people who dream big dreams and take great actions, and stop taking advice from broke, unhappy people. Don't be afraid to cut ties with some people and let them go." *–David Wood*

4. Be selfless and constantly give, give, give to your network. The returns will come back tenfold.

"It's been really beneficial spending time adding value to other people. Then people in my network add value back. The more I reach out and help, the more help I get." *–Billy Murphy*

5. Build your team. Every single expert has a coach, and if you want great results, you should as well!

"Find somebody who will work with you, challenge you, and give you guidance. Find somebody who's been down the road before, somebody who can really mentor you and help you develop. It's not just about growing your income; it's about growing yourself. You need to make sure you're paying attention to that." *–John Murphy*

CHAPTER 4: BUILD THE FINANCIAL FOUNDATION

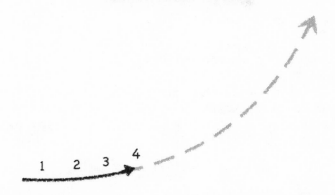

Don't launch your tower without a great foundation.
—Ann Wilson

Wealth takes time to accumulate and build, and unless you have a strong foundation, it won't last. As a result, this is step #4 on your way to wealth.

A strong base is important because it's where all growth begins. Without it, your financial house could crumble at any time. This is why lottery winners often end up broke shortly after winning becoming rich—they don't have the foundation in place.

> Know what you're doing with your money. If you can't manage what you've got, you can't manage more. When you get your foundational money habits down, you'll be able to expand.
> *—Ann Wilson*

A strong foundation consists not only of the right mindset and environment, but also of a proper plan of action, the right habits and protection, and a strong financial position from which to grow. Although these things are not the most exciting pieces of wealth-building, they are completely necessary to in order to both create and keep massive wealth.

Delete Debt

> Getting out and staying out of debt is key. Debt is the biggest barrier, a parasite to wealth.
> *—Ann Wilson*

The most common financial challenge that people need to overcome is also the first major financial goal: get out of debt!

Nearly 70% of American families carry debt, but they're not alone. The wealthy experts themselves shared countless stories of how they, as well, had gotten in the debt trap early on in their careers. Their debt grew and grew until they finally made the decision and commitment to turn their finances around.

> Debt is stupid. It robs you of your options. It holds you back from growth. If somebody is telling you that you need debt, ask the questions, 'What is your value? What is your net worth?' There are two categories of people claiming you need debt: people who are selling debt and people who don't have money.
> *—Chris Locurto*

The good news is that you can overcome massive debt. Jason Vitug was $78,000 in debt at age 25. Justin Williams found his business in a $120,000 hole shortly after starting it. Both David Weliver and I were able to overcome $80,000 of debt in just a few years.

The key elements of overcoming the exorbitant debt levels discussed on the podcast were:

- Commitment and focus.

  o When trying to overcome a lot of debt, your focus should be solely on that debt. Every extra penny should go towards that one goal. With this focus, you can escape the debt trap much quicker.

- Stop acquiring new debt.

Chapter 4: Build a Financial Foundation

- o This is key. The reason people can't get out of debt is that they keep adding new debt.

- Sacrifice temporarily.

  - o David Weliver went above and beyond to escape being in debt. He halved his rent, got a 2nd part-time job, and paid every extra penny towards his debts. In 3 years, his $80,000 of debt was erased.

- Have a plan and pick the strategy that best appeals to you. Two common strategies are the *debt snowball* and *debt stacking* methods.

  - o Debt Snowball: Pay the minimum on all debts, and then pay as much as you can on the loan with the lowest balance. Once you pay off that loan, move on to pay extra on the new lowest balance loan. This strategy gets you in motion. You can quickly see progress by having one less bill in the mail each month.

  - o Debt Stacking: Pay the minimum on all debts, and pay as much as you can on the highest interest rate loan you have. This strategy is good because you pay less interest by getting rid of the highest interest debts first.

You can't be completely free with the burden of debt hanging over your head, so stay focused and delete the debt as fast as possible. Then you'll be able to take on more risk and grow.

Financial Foundation Checklist	Financial Goal	Complete?
#1	Get Out of Debt	
#2	Emergency Fund	

Cast a Safety Net

The biggest mistake beginners make is not building a cash cushion.
—Brittney Castro

The wealthy believe that cash is king, and for good reason. There are two things that you can guarantee will occur—unexpected emergencies and investment opportunities. You should be prepared for both.

So how much cash should you have on hand? It depends on whom you ask.

While you're getting out of debt, you need to have something. I recommend $1,000. It is not a whole lot of money but will take care of a lot of things. After you get the debt out of your life, start to save up for a big emergency because something is going to happen. Look at your real expenses. If you have to exist on the bare minimum, how much would that be? Multiply that by 3-to-6 months, and you've got your number.
—Steve Stewart

Patrick Bet-David, on the other hand, holds ten years' worth of cash on hand for potential opportunities and recommends others to have at least twelve months saved up. But regardless of your cash position, make sure you have enough stashed away to handle the unexpected events in your life. Not only do you need an emergency fund, but you need other protection as well.

I'm conscious of looking for protection first: insurances, legal documents (will, trust, etc.). I usually ask my clients, *Are you going to retire tomorrow?* The answer is typically *No.* My next question is *Are you going to get into a car accident tomorrow?* The answer to that is *I have no idea.* You have to protect yourself from what could happen today versus worrying about retirement, which may be 10-20 years off.

The analogy I use all of the time is this. The safest vehicle in the world is a racecar. What other vehicle can you be going 180-200 mph, slam into a wall, and walk away from that crash? The reason a racecar can go so fast is because of the protection. So you must have that protection, whether insurances or if you're talking about managing risk in your investments. Then, when opportunities arise, you'll be ready.
—Ryan Michler

Chapter 4: Build a Financial Foundation

If you have the right foundation, protection, and habits, then you, too, can go as fast as possible—take risk—and know that you will still be able to recover if things don't work out as planned. This is how you'll be able to build a fortune quickly.

Save, Don't Spend

The formula for wealth is quite simple . . .

> Spend less than you earn and invest the difference wisely.
> —*Todd Tresidder, sharing 'the wealth equation'*

The part of this equation that is easiest to change is how much you spend. Yet this is where so many people get into trouble.

> The best advice I ever received was, *spend to live*. Cover the basics (housing, food, transportation), but spend your money on experiences, not things.
> —*Jason Vitug*

	Non-Wealthy	**Wealthy**
What They Value:	Short-term satisfaction	"I want my money to buy my freedom." —*Rob Berger*

> It's not how much money you make that makes the difference; it's how much money you spend. The hardest thing in the world is keeping expenses low. You need to focus more so on what's going out.
> —*Josh Brown*

After all, it's not how much you make, it is how much you *keep* that matters. Whether your income is $500,000 or $50,000, you can't get ahead unless you live below your means.

The common person has what JD Roth called 'lifestyle inflation.' As earnings go up, so too do expenses. The best way to make progress in this area is by avoiding emotional—i.e. regrettable—purchases.

Make Money, Live Wealthy

Get rid of the SOS (shiny object syndrome) mentality—the feeling of having to go out and buy stuff.
—Mike Kawula

Mindy Crary said that these impulse decisions are the biggest mistake people make. One way to avoid SOS or lifestyle inflation is what I call 'The Honeymoon Rule.' Here are the rules:

- For any item you want that costs more than $100 (set whatever amount you want), decide whether or not it is a good purchase—but don't buy it yet.

- If deemed 'good', wait 30 days.

- If it is still a good decision after 30 days, then by all means buy it. If not, then don't.

By adding a time delay to a purchase, you take the emotions out of it. We often see something as a *need* in the moment, when in reality it is only a *want*. The results of emotional purchases most often a cause of both buyer's remorse and an empty bank account.

The important point of all this is to be cognizant of the decisions you're making and to make logical decisions that help get you what you want (true wealth).

Track your spending and know where your money is going. If you sit down and look at these numbers, you will realize where you can make significant savings. This will allow you to gather more wealth early on because you can use that money to make more money instead of spending money freely.
—Patrick Schulte, investor, traveler, co-author of Live on the Margin

Don't just track your expenses, but do something about them. Cut out anything unnecessary and put the savings from these cuts to good use elsewhere. Mike Kawula suggests finding a way to reduce your expenses by 20%—there is always a way. Then invest that money back into yourself, and you'll be in a much better position down the road.

Chapter 4: Build a Financial Foundation

Once you identify where your money is going, you'll see some red flags, but you'll also see that the majority of your necessities are tied up in just a few areas.

> Housing accounts for one-third of your budget; transportation accounts for one-sixth. Combined, that is half of your budget. If you can cut your cost of spending in these areas, you can make a big impact.
> —*JD Roth*

So what exactly does this mean? It means that our focus should be on the big-ticket items—income, housing and transportation expenses, and taxes. These areas will have the greatest impact. A 5% change in any of them has a much bigger impact than saving a dollar here and there.

	<u>Non-Wealthy</u>	<u>Wealthy</u>
Save Money by:	Cutting Coupons	Trimming big expenses: housing, transportation, taxes
	Stop Drinking $5 Lattes	Making things automatic so you don't (know you) have the money to spend.

What is really important to you? What do you want your money to buy? The reason this matters is because your personal money goals will ensure that you use your money toward things that will actually bring you what you want—time, freedom, peace of mind, unforgettable experiences.

> When you save money, you are buying future freedom.
> —*JD Roth*

To change your habits, think about your expenses differently. 'Time is money,' as the saying goes, but money is also time. The more money you have, the more time you have—and that is the greatest asset in the world.

> That's why it's so important for young people to save. Everyone focuses on spreadsheets. If you save this much, over time it will grow to be a million dollars. That's all mathematically accurate, but that's not

how people think. In reality, what the chart shows you is how much of your own free time you can get back. If you have enough money, you have all of your time. If you don't, you have to continue to work. If you don't save early on, you're not looking at a smaller number at the end; you're looking at years that you need to continue to work.

—Jim Wang, successful entrepreneur, personal finance expert

In order for Jim to feel both comfortable and secure when he quit his job, he felt he needed to save three years worth of *time* to see if he could get his business up and operating. If it didn't work out before the three years was up, he could still return to the workforce and everything would be fine. This time allowed him to build a stellar business that quickly grew to be worth much more than his previous job.

To buy yourself more time, you not only want to reduce your expenses, but you really want to simplify your money.

You have to focus on two things: automating and separating your savings. You want to put your savings on autopilot, whether that's auto-withdrawal or auto-deposit—some way to make the savings process happen automatically without you physically moving money from one account to another. This can happen with your 401k, ROTH IRA, or a simple savings account. The key phrase for people who automated their savings is, "I didn't miss the money."

The second aspect is separation. Look for ways to shield your money from yourself. Put it in places where it's hard for you to get it. For example, there are tax penalties and interest involved with removing that money early from your 401k or ROTH IRA. Another idea is putting it in a savings account that is not attached to your checking account.

— Philip Taylor, CPA, personal finance expert, PTMoney.com

Saving is not necessarily a fun thing to do, so you have to make it as easy as possible on yourself. Set up your funds in a way that you don't even touch the money. Once you don't have it there for you to waste, you start to really build your fund. Remember the key phrase—"I didn't miss the money." Simplify your life and your savings, and you'll be well on your way.

Chapter 4: Build a Financial Foundation

*If you have high expenses, you'll find yourself on the treadmill of life.
You're going to be running hard and getting nowhere.*
—*Rob Berger, attorney, founder of DoughRoller.net*

The Money Plan

*The first step is awareness of your financial situation. The next step is
creating a plan, and then taking action on it.*
—*Jason Vitug*

Self-awareness is key. You need not only to assess your skills and emotions, but to really know your finances inside and out.

Become the CFO (chief financial officer) of your own life.
—*JD Roth*

Remember, you can't fix what you don't know, so be a pro at what is going on with your money. The more you know, the more obvious the problems and solutions become.

A great free tool—suggested numerous times by my podcast experts—is Mint.com. It tracks all of your expenses in one place, so you can get a clear picture on where your money is going. Numerous guests also suggested creating a balance sheet of your money.

*I would suggest pulling out a sheet of paper and creating a balance
sheet: here's what I own, here's what I owe. Do a simple budget and
have a sensible understanding of where your assets are. Look for more
ways to put money into your portfolio, into your retirement, into your
emergency fund.*

*It's your responsibility. The decisions that you make on those changes
will dictate which direction the rest of your life takes.*
—*Tom Basso*

Ann Wilson states the importance of not focusing solely on your income, but instead trying to really grow your *worth*. That's important. Your worth takes into account more variables than just how much money you're bringing in.

When you write things down and see where your money is going, you'll be able to clearly see the errors you've been making and make rational decisions more easily. Even if you don't feel that saving is a challenge for you, this process will help you see the big picture.

From there, create a money plan. How are you going to get where you want to go financially? What actions will be necessary, and what do you need to focus on first to help get you there?

> Get a plan. There is a power in having a plan because it gives you clarity on what you need to do and what actions you need to take.
> —*Brittney Castro*

Most people want to chase the money and try to get rich quickly, but the fastest and smoothest path is often the long way around. Instead of rushing blindly after more money, start by creating a roadmap to your true destination.

The best plan is one that aligns your priorities with your goals.

Finances are very personal, so your specific situation and interests may vary from those of others; however, consider the list of financial priorities that many have suggested below (note, Chapter 8 is all about investing, so any terms you're not familiar with will be clarified in that section)—

1. Debt minimums

2. Minimum emergency fund ($1,000)

3. Max out corporate 401k match (if available)

4. Get out of high-interest debt

5. Medium emergency fund ($10,000)

6. Roth IRA (Individual Retirement Account)

7. Max out remaining retirement options (Additional 401(k), Traditional or SEP IRA)

8. Complete emergency fund (six months of expenses)

9. Pay extra on low-interest debt

10. Taxable investing account

There are other things you can consider based on your goals (i.e. children's funds, larger cash fund), skills (expected investment returns), and the interest rates on your debts, but this list of priorities gives you a good starting place. If you have a large expense coming up (wedding, car, vacation), then you should include that on your list. If you have a family, you may want to make having a larger emergency fund a higher priority.

Regardless, the major point is that the best way to wealth is to take a methodical and structured approach. Building your finances and understanding every aspect of your financial situation can be overwhelming, so the best way to master it is by taking just one step at a time. By using a structured approach, you'll be better prepared, pay less in interest, and take advantage of taxes and free money.

This plan will change over time as your priorities and goals change, but the key is to combine your goals and priorities with some milestones and steps of action. You don't have to know every single movement you'll make from here until you're a multimillionaire, but you *should* know are what the final image looks like, and the first few steps you're going to take to get there. Then—get into motion.

Summary

A. Awareness is key.

Nobody cares more than you do about your finances, so you need to become your own CFO. The more you know about your habits and where your money is going, the easier it'll be to fix any leaks.

Start by creating a simple balance sheet to show what your worth is and whether it's growing each month. Putting the numbers down on paper and adding up your expenses can really open your eyes to some red flags that need to be addressed.

Do a balance sheet. What are your assets and liabilities? That's where net worth starts. Where you can, focus on growing your worth rather than your income.
—*Ann Wilson*

B. Debt is stupid.

You can't be financially free with debt. This is the biggest barrier to wealth, and it needs to be a top financial priority on your way to riches.

Stay out of debt. It is easier to swim to paradise with your head above water, not having to deal with the added weight of debt around your neck.
—*Steve Stewart*

Compound interest works for you (investing) or against you (debt). You decide.

C. Cash is king.

The only thing you can count on is that the unexpected will happen when you least expect it. Prepare for it by building an emergency fund.

You should have a substantial emergency fund; start with at least six months worth of expenses and be completely debt free.
—*Anton Ivanov*

Your safety stash is valuable for three major reasons:

1) Peace of mind.

2) The expected/unexpected troubles.

3) Opportunities that arise.

D. When you save money, you buy your future freedom.

Spend your money buying assets instead of spending it on useless expenses or getting into debt.
—*Anton Ivanov, entrepreneur, investor*

Chapter 4: Build a Financial Foundation

The wealthy buy assets, experiences, and time . . . not things. As mentioned earlier, time is money, but money is also time. The more you save, the more future freedom you'll have.

Housing, transportation, and taxes make up the majority of your expenses. Trim these, and they'll have a much larger impact on your outgoing funds than focusing on the small expenses.

Another key is to make things simple. Automate where possible and separate your accounts so that you don't have to see them. Remember—out of sight, out of mind. Get things set up and running on autopilot and avoid emotional spending. Once you do this, your net worth will grow on autopilot.

> In the logical sense, wealth is three things: 1) solid credit score, 2) an income stream that allows you to take more risk, and 3) savings. Savings gives you a lot of strength, flexibility, and control. Savings are what give you the most powerful answer in the world.
> —*Patrick Bet-David*

E. The wealthy have a structured plan that helps propel them to their goals.

The wealthy have a plan. Do you?

A plan is a combination of your goals, priorities, and action steps that will get you to your destination.

The quickest way to wealth is not immediately taking action. Rather, it is in thinking about where you're going, preparing how it is you're going to get there, and then taking massive action.

Action Items

1. See exactly how I paid off $80,000 worth of debt and more at MakeMoneyLiveWealthy.com/chapter4, including examples of the priorities you should focus on financially, and much more.

2. Make getting out of debt your number one financial priority. Stop adding new debt! That is the first key step to getting out of the debt-trap once and for all.

3. Set up a separate savings account for your Emergency Fund. This should be separate from your checking account, and you should not touch it unless it is absolutely necessary.

Start with $1,000. If you have a family, you'll likely want to quickly move up to having at least $5,000-10,000 saved up as your next milestone. Many suggest that you should ultimately have six months of expenses set aside for family emergencies.

4. Sign up for a free account at mint.com. There you can link all of your accounts, and you can track where your money goes, identify trends, and make goals. It is an amazing free tool suggested numerous times by the experts.

Check your credit card charges every month. You'll often find charges for subscriptions you had forgotten to cancel, mystery charges you didn't even know about (bank fees), or overcharges (possibly from a bar/restaurant).

5. Identify 10% of your expenses—things you can live without—and cut them. See what happens for a month. I'm sure you won't even notice their absence, but you will notice the increase in money. Put that "found" money to good use by investing in yourself—your education, career, network, wealth (debt or emergency fund)—or invest it and let it grow!

"Every single person can cut his or her expenses by 10-20%. Find a way to do it." –*Robert Farrington,*

CHAPTER 5: FIND CLARITY

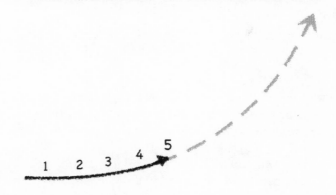

What I've learned from the wealthy over the years is different from what most of us think. When you really want to get somewhere fast, the first thing you need to do is go, go, go, right?

Actually, the answer is *No*.

The best step toward success isn't the obvious one—it isn't motion or quick movement. What you need to do is to stop and get a firm grasp on where you're headed and why.

Non-Wealthy

Try to Get Rich Quick

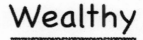

Fail

Wealthy

1. Take Control
2. Build Foundation
3. Find Clarity

Slowing down and actually stopping for a few seconds is so hard for many of us to do. If we don't keep busy, we feel like we're wasting time. In a world surrounded by never-ending communication, multiple distractions, and a record amount of ADHD diagnoses, we literally don't know how to stop.

Our goal shouldn't be the act of being busy, but rather getting the results you want—and that starts with being purposeful about where you're headed and how you intend to get there. Stopping for a moment allows you to work smart, not hard.

Clarity is power.
- *David Wood*

If you remember just five lessons from this book, remember this one: clarity is power. This step is critical because it focuses you on the things that matter and heads down the correct path. It puts you on a direct line to success.

Without clarity, you will run into many dead ends, and this with ultimately cost you a lot more time, headaches, and heartache along the way.

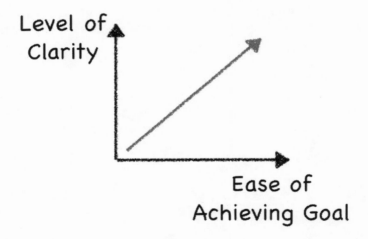

The more clearly you define a problem, the more obvious and easy the solution becomes. Opportunities and resources are all around us, but until you have that clear vision, you will not be able to see them.

In addition, having that focused mission keeps you consistently striving toward your goal and prevents you from getting sidetracked along the way. The worst thing you can do is work hard and put in the hours to move towards something that isn't even going to make you happy in the end anyway.

Chapter 5: Find Clarity

It's a journey. In my own journey, there was a lot of searching, a lot of studying, a lot of self-analysis and plotting the things that I want to be.
—John Murphy

It starts with defining what it is that you really want.

<u>The Balanced Life</u>

	<u>Non-Wealthy</u>	<u>Wealthy</u>
The Secret to Having True Wealth:	Money	Balance

As with everything in life, there needs to be a balance. We are happiest when our work, life, money, and relationships are balanced in the correct proportion to our desires.

The most common balance we seek is between our work and our personal life, when, in fact, these things should blend together. Work is a key part of your life.

I think it's artificial to think that we put on one hat when we go to work and then we're somebody else when we come home on a weekend. It stems from the way we usually frame work: 'Thank god, it's Friday. I don't have to go to work tomorrow.'

We frame retirement the same way. It conveys the idea that as soon as I get enough money saved up for myself, then I can quit this stinking job and do something I love.

But what if you figure out how to make money doing what you really love? Then retirement loses its appeal; Friday loses its appeal.

Not that I don't enjoy the weekend. People who'd follow me around would scratch their head, not sure if I'm working or playing because it looks so much the same.
—Dan Miller

Make Money, Live Wealthy

Things in your life should flow together so that you can be yourself —all-out, all of the time.

Your business is what you do, not who you are.

Some people become so consumed with business that they become desperate to be successful, desperate to avoid mistakes. What they end up messing up on is life, which is what it's all about, after all.

You have to be focused on being balanced in career, financials, spiritual, physical, intellect, family, and social relationships. You need a balance with the people who are partners in your life.

It's receiving *and* pouring out. You can't sit there and receive and not give anything out. The whole wheel is vitally important. It's a balancing act.
—*Chris Locurto*

It's all about that balance. JV Crum asked a strong and important question: "What area of your life are you putting on hold?" Consider that question seriously as it'll help you identify which area you should focus on to move towards more balance.

Dennis Cummins learned six human needs from one of his inspirations and mentors, Tony Robbins. These six needs are certainty, excitement, significance, intimacy/love, growth, and contribution.

The goal is to find something in your life that will satisfy as many of those six needs as possible. What will make you feel fulfilled and take care of your basic needs? What is really going to bring joy into your life? If you can figure that out, you will know where to focus.
—*Dr. Dennis Cummins*

It's the simple things that matter the most—health, relationships, the feeling of significance. What is money without these things?

Complete happiness comes from being balanced in the important areas of our lives. Identify the gaps in what you want in your life, and fill them.

Chapter 5: Find Clarity

If you can get to that place and understand that your business is what
you do, not who you are, then you can be truly wealthy.
—Chris Locurto

<u>Your Dream Lifestyle</u>

Balance and lifestyle go hand in hand.

Many believe that if they find the right job, they'll have both happiness and wealth. These same people go out and find a career that they're interested in and try it, but it doesn't work out. Why? Because it doesn't allow them to live the lifestyle that they want. They have to spend less time with their kids, or they can't travel like they want, or they aren't making enough money to live the life that they want to outside of work.

The trick is to begin with the end in mind. Your job or career should fit into the lifestyle you want, not the other way around. This is very important.

Think of the lifestyle you want to live today, tomorrow, and throughout retirement, and base your decisions on these lifestyle goals. There are financial goals, but it's important to think about the quality of life you want to live and factor that into the type of investments you're willing to make, your savings plan, and the budgeting of your personal financial life.
—Jason Vitug

Once you're clear on the picture of your ideal life, you need to figure out what kinds of investments—in both time and effort—you're willing to make to get there. Then fill in the details of how much to save and invest and what type of income you need—if any—to get to your goal and be able to live that lifestyle.

Patrick Schulte and his wife created their vision. They wanted to be free to sail around the world (even though they had never sailed before in their lives). After a few beers one night, they decided to see that dream through. They worked to put themselves in a financial position where they could leave their careers and sail off on their dream journey. They've been living that same lifestyle for ten years—even now with a family—with no signs of slowing down soon.

Think about it: when we get jealous of other people's careers, we're not really jealous of the specific job responsibilities or the money as much as we're jealous of the lifestyle they get to enjoy with it, right? Figure this out, and you'll avoid chasing many dead ends on your path to true wealth.

> First, focus on the end result. Reverse engineer what you want. Fast-forward a year or two and think about what you really want, and what you value. I defined what I wanted and put the pieces in place. I found the right people to complement my businesses and teams so that I knew that I would be able to continue building and growing the business without having my time attached to it. It's important to be able to scale things and be able to figure out big opportunities that are not attached to your time.
> —Peter Voogd

Design first, then backtrack the steps needed to get you there. Gain that clarity and then go after it with all you've got!

> The real art of wealth is playing all-out, passionately designing that lifestyle, and knowing with clarity what it is that truly juices us, rather than what we believe defines us in society.
> —Ann Wilson

Money's Role

> People don't want to get rich. They want to get happy!
> —JD Roth

A bad goal is to make more money just for the sake of being rich. This is fine to *want*, but money is not what you *really* want. It is not the solution to your problems.

> Quit thinking of money as the means to your goals. *You* are the means to your goals. Money is just a tool.
> —Mindy Crary

Money doesn't create a life—it supports one. To many, money is everything. But to many of the experts interviewed, it *used to be* everything. Entrepreneur Erlend Bakke, like me, was one of those people.

Chapter 5: Find Clarity

I think I had the wrong kind of programming— the programming from movies and society where you're trained to go, 'Okay, once I achieve this I'll be happy.' I was hypnotized by the idea that if I only make enough money, everything else is going to fall into place.
—Erlend Bakke, bestselling author of Never Work Again

But as we mature and learn, we realize money's true role in our lives. It is only a piece of a much bigger equation.

The amount of money you have, or how much you make in the long run, is often a scorecard for how much value you're providing. It is a source of motivation and can give you the ability to live the life that you want to live. It is an important tool, but it's not the single goal. That is important to learn as early in life as possible.

So how much money is enough?

In Malcolm Gladwell's latest book, *David and Goliath*, he featured some research done on families. The average family income for happiness is $75,000.
—Erlend Bakke

Anything more than that isn't absolutely necessary. More than that is about 'wants', not 'needs.'

Many experts shared stories of how they chased money in their careers, only to find out that wasn't what they were really looking for.

After college, I was a young professional trying to find my way in the business world. I told myself, if I only made $35,000, I would be happy and sufficient. I made it and it was not enough. I made more, and it still wasn't enough.

Then I realized it's not really about the money. For me, wealth is being able to not worry about the day-to-day expenses. It's the ability to follow your passion and build a foundation of financial independence that can serve you and your family for the years to come.
—Erez Katz, serial entrepreneur, co-founder and CEO of Lucena Research

Make Money, Live Wealthy

You see, the reason why money is not the goal is because it is not the end. There's a reason behind why you want money, and that's what we want to get to. For Erez, the real goals were having the security of being able to provide for his family without stress and the ability to follow his passion. Money is just something that allows him to achieve that peace of mind and freedom.

> More important than making money is discovering what you want to do with that money. Making money for the sake of making money is a dead end.

> When I was young, I just wanted to make a lot of money, but there was no goal, no purpose for that money. Now, I consider a person wealthy when he has enough money to do what he wants to do. I use money to buy myself time. I value experiences much more than possessions. You can always make more money, but you can't make more time.
> —*Patrick Schulte*

By realizing what the goal really is, you give yourself stronger reasons to make the right decisions. Making more money isn't as important as having more time to do what you wish.

So what is the purpose of your money then? When you're about to spend a lot of money on something, think of the big picture. Is this going to help get you what you *really* want? If the answer is *yes*, then by all means, spend away.

> I want my money to buy my freedom. The most important thing it can buy—more than a fancy car or clothes or a vacation—is the freedom to do what I love to do.
> —*Rob Berger*

Define Goals

What do you really want? I think people really only want four things:

1) Financial freedom or wealth.

2) Health for themselves and their family.

3) Great relationships and love in their lives.

4) Happiness.

What will give you those things? You just have to spend some time
meditating, journaling, and writing down a list.
—Dr. Dennis Cummins

Dream big! Don't hold anything back. Don't make insignificant goals—or
small ones because you don't think you can achieve larger ones. The surefire
way to *not* achieve something is to never believe that you can do it.

If your dreams don't scare you, then they're not big enough. I set my
goals every year so that I have about 50/50 chances of getting them. If
I ever got all of my goals, I'd be mortified. I'd say, 'Why did I set my
sights so low?'
—Dan Miller

The reason making goals—and especially making them very clear—is so
important is because those goals and visions pull us toward our destination. It
goes back to mindset—thinking and believing as the rich do.

In my world, my goals are success, fulfillment, happiness, safety, and
health. That's what I'm attracting into my world.

If we keep our focus on the end result and trust the process,
everything will work out along those lines. We don't have to know
how we're getting to the destination; we just know that we will. That
end is going to force the means.
—Coach Mike Basevic

The end will force the means, so be sure that end is a huge dream, an enormous goal. Then, believe and achieve.

<u>The Big Why</u>

> Everybody has a why, a purpose. The million-dollar nugget is figuring out what that is. When you do, the whole game changes. Part of the process of being an amazing entrepreneur or building that ideal lifestyle is pulling out your reason from within you.
> *—Peter Voogd*

A 'why' is your purpose for doing what you do. It's the reason behind your goals and the driving force behind the decisions that you make. Why do you do what you do? Why do you want the things you want?

> Defining my 'why' was the most important step in my career—getting crystal clear about the *why* and not being so obsessed with the *how* and the *what*.
> *—John Murphy*

As we develop and grow, our 'why' changes along with us. David Wood said his why has grown immensely, and it's now to make a global impact and leave a legacy. Matt McWilliams does everything for one reason—to change the world.

> I am a world changer, and so are you. It's a philosophy that I developed. If we aren't born to change the world, what purpose are we born for? Whatever reason you serve on this earth, if it's not to have a significant impact, then you serve no purpose. Everybody is here for a purpose. I believe that our purpose is so much bigger than so many people think.
> *—Matt McWilliams*

The reason identifying your purpose is so important is that there will be many challenges along the way that will tempt you to give up and go back to doing what's easiest in the here and now. No truly honest wealthy person will tell you that it'll be all rainbows and sunshine. There will be times when you are really tested, and the only way to get through those times is to have a 'why' that is big enough to overcome those obstacles!

Chapter 5: Find Clarity

It is important to have a mission statement, a clear guiding purpose that moves you so much that you're willing to sacrifice and do the hard things to get to where you want to go.
—JD Roth

If you have a mission, it will not only lead you through the major challenges, but also to lead you to so many amazing and unexpected places.

I never had a plan in life, but I had a mission. How can my life be an adventure? How can I be the best human being I can possibly be? How can I learn as much as I want? What is the meaning of life? How can I end up at the end of my life without any regrets? Is there a God?

I followed my star, and it led me to Louis Mobley [his mentor, founder of the IBM Executive School]. Everything in my life has been a series of 'happy accidents,' which are by-products or trailing indicators of living life for a higher purpose.
—August Turak

Finding your 'why' gives intentionality to your actions. When you find your true purpose and act according to it, the universe rewards you with the happy accidents August talks about. You'll have focus and a clear mission, and you'll be less easily knocked off course. You'll be aware of the abundance of opportunities that appear in your life to help you accomplish your goals.

Summary

A. Clarity is power.

Step #1 of the Ultimate Success Formula is clarity. Know the outcome of exactly what you want and say, *Yes!*
—David Wood

You don't climb behind the wheel of your car until you know where you're going to go. The wealthy know their direction and know their goals—and that gives them absolute power.

The clearer the vision and mission, the easier the road will be along the way. Clarity about who you are, what you want, and why you want it does three things:

1) It keeps you focused on your mission with certainty and helps you achieve your goals more quickly.

2) It brings out your greatest skills and interests, leading to increased wealth and happiness.

3) It encourages you to believe in your own mission and in yourself, the greatest hurdles you can overcome.

Even so, things don't become completely clear until you get into motion. It's important to look inward and analyze yourself, but then you need act on it— try it out to see for yourself if it's the correct path for you.

Clarity comes through engagement, not through thought.
—*Kate Northrup*

B. True wealth comes from being balanced in the way that suits you.

Money is only one aspect of wealth. Wealth is a well-balanced, happy life.
—*Chris Locurto*

Keep things in perspective and never let one area dominate your time and energy. The key to wealth is this never-ending balance of all of the important areas of your life.

Also, don't look for 'work-life balance.' The truly wealthy fit their work into their life and their life into their work seamlessly.

C. A secret to finding your dream career is to find something that fits into the lifestyle you dream of.

We often think we're jealous of other people's careers, but what we're really jealous of is either the fulfillment they get out of the job or the lifestyle it allows them to enjoy (or both!).

Chapter 5: Find Clarity

By working backward, you can move forward in the quickest way. Start by figuring out the lifestyle you want to enjoy, then fill in the details of what you can do to have that lifestyle.

D. Money is a tool, not *the* goal.

> Having a lot of money is being rich, but wealth is when you have an abundance of both money and meaning.
> —*Hugh Kimura, foreign exchange trader, founder of TradingHeroes.com*

Money isn't the main focus, but it is a very important tool that allows you to live the life you want to live. It's very important, however, to evaluate what the purpose for making more money is for you. Remember, there is a reason behind the drive to get rich. Always keep sight of the bigger picture, and use money for whatever that picture is.

> The mindset of true wealth gives every dollar a purpose.
> —*Steve Stewart*

Money is much better spent to buy you time, freedom, experience and happiness than it is to acquire 'things.'

E. The wealthy dream big.

> Before you build something, you must design it. You need to have a design and intentionality to your life; that's a very important part of creating the success that you want.
> —*Jon Gordon*

Dreaming of achieving something is a prerequisite to actually getting there. You need goals in order to draw the road map of *how* to get there.

> A truly wealthy guy knows what he wants and goes out and gets it. You should have goals; you should always be working toward something.
> —*Patrick Schulte*

Don't just dream—dream *big*. You should set your goals high enough that you surely do not achieve them all.

F. Purpose is wealth.

> Whatever you want to do, it has got to come with a purpose.
> —*Larry Stevens*

Everyone has a 'why'—a driving force behind the decisions that one makes. If you find that *why*, you can use it to your advantage and overcome any obstacle. The stronger and clearer your vision, the better off you will be because challenges are inevitable.

> When you find your true passion, you discover clarity. You can say
> in a single sentence, 'This is my purpose.'

> During the growth stage, you'll face a lot of challenges; you'll get a
> lot of prunes. They seem like setbacks, but they make you stronger
> and better.

> Everybody wants to dream, but nobody wants to grind. It's during
> the grind that we become stronger. Your purpose must be greater
> than your challenges; when it is, you overcome them.
> —*Jon Gordon*

If you live in a way that is true to you and your purpose, you'll be rewarded in more ways than you can imagine.

Action Items

1. Take the free life balance tests and download the goal worksheets at MakeMoneyLiveWealthy.com/chapter5.

2. Identify your current balance score for each important area of your life. (Source: Zig Ziglar's Wheel of Life)

   a. Rank the below areas in order of importance to you and score yourself on a scale of 1-10 (10 being excellent) for each area.

b. Which parts of the wheel need the most attention? What is one action that you can perform in each area to improve your score? Focus on one small step at a time, one area at a time.

3. Create your dream lifestyle.

    a. What does it look like? Where are you living? What is your schedule like? Who are you with? When and how do you work?

    b. What are you willing to invest (time and effort) to help you get there? This will help determine the amount of money and/or type of income you need to achieve this lifestyle.

4. Figure out money's role in your life. Why do you really want to make more money? What is the result of more money, and what will it bring you?

5. Define what true wealth is to you.

    a. What is truly important? What do you *really* want? Refer back to the definitions of true wealth in the Introduction to complete your own version.

    b. Identify your level of personal wealth using the free tool at MakeMoneyLiveWealthy.com/chapter5.

6. Create your goals for the different time frames. This takes time, but it is very important. Write these down and make a calendar reminder to review them on a monthly basis.

Big Picture	What are some big dream goals you'd like to achieve in your life?
5-Year	In five years, what would you like to have accomplished?
1-Year	In 12 months, what will your life look like? What is the big thing you need to do within a year to get you towards your 5-year goal?
6 Months	What is one thing you will change in your life in the next six months? What do you need to accomplish to get you where you want to go?
1 Month	What is the one thing you need to do this month to get you toward your six-month goal?

7. Figure out your ONE word. What is it?

"There's one word that's meant for you. There's one word that's meant to serve as a driving force for your life to give you clarity. You have this word that is meant to help you be your best this year.

Each year, pick a different word. It gives you meaning and mission, and it allows you to say, 'Am I really living this word this year?' When we live our word, we become so much more powerful." *—Jon Gordon*

CHAPTER 6: CRAFT YOUR DREAM CAREER

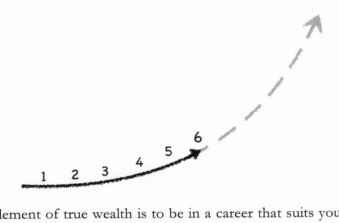

The next element of true wealth is to be in a career that suits your goals. The wealthy know where they want to be in life, and they figure out the best way to get there. The best way is by doing work that they love.

> You've got two jobs in this life. Be a good person and do what you love.
> —Ryan Holiday (on the best advice he ever received)

Two jobs. That's it. Be a good person and do what you love. I'm going to guess that you're doing the first already, but are you really doing what you love? Remember the statistic: 70% of people hate what they're doing or are completely uninspired at work.

> This is even crazier—people are in action doing something they don't like, getting results that suck, and they're not doing anything about it. They're trapped. They just keep doing it because that is what they know.
> —David Wood

If you see the majority of people doing something, it's not always a bad idea to go in the opposite direction. You don't have to be someone who hates his or her work. It is key to recognize that you can combine some of your passions and your work to create something that excites you.

<u>Pursue a Passion</u>

Don't just work for a paycheck. If you have a passion or a dream,
there's a way of integrating that with what you're doing.
—Ruben Rojas

The experts interviewed on my podcast are doing the work they want to do—
every single one of them. They no longer do what is expected of them, but
they do what is in the best interests of themselves and their families. In order
to live out your passions, sometimes it's necessary to go against the grain.

Don't get hung up on what you think is expected of you or what's
going to make you the most money or anything like that. Understand
what it is that's going to drive you; what is it that's going to motivate
you?
—John Murphy

Peter Voogd shared the story of his entrepreneurial beginnings. He had so
much social pressure around him to go the 'normal' route that he originally
veered in that direction. He did what everyone else wanted him to do before
he'd finally had enough and began making his own decisions.

When you do things based on other people's opinions of you or other
people's lack of ambition or beliefs, you'll always feel regrets. If you do
things based on others' opinions, it's challenging to have peace of
mind and be happy and excited about your future.
—Peter Voogd

We've been trained to believe that it's acceptable—and normal—to not enjoy
what we do for a living, because so few are actually excited by their work.
We've seen so many heading in a certain direction, so we feel like the best
option for us is to do exactly the same. Just know that there is another way.

Create something that's really exciting. There are other people who
share your interest. Do the introspective work now, and follow your
passion.
—Kathleen Kingsbury

Make Money, Live Wealthy

Being wealthy is living a life of passion and purpose, yet so many don't even know what their passions are—let alone live them out.

> Seventy-five percent of the people for whom I've done life plans say, 'I don't have a clue!' It's not shocking to me because that's what I do for a living, but other people are surprised to realize they don't know what they're passionate about. That's because they have never spent any time saying, 'What do I really love to do? What gets me excited every day?'
> —*Chris Locurto*

Spend some time answering those questions. For Chris, what gets him excited is changing lives, helping others to become better individuals, and showing them how to grow their businesses and themselves. When asked the number one reason for his success, Chris said it was because he found and followed these passions.

On Doing What You Love:

Non-Wealthy	Wealthy
"It's not realistic."	It is "the secret to my success." – *Chris Locurto*
"It's work. It's supposed to suck."	"The more you enjoy it, the more success you have." – *Hugh Kimura*
"It's too late to follow my passion."	"It doesn't matter if somebody's 18 or 88. Tomorrow's going to be a new day." – *Dan Miller*

We all have passions, and we all have a purpose. What is yours? What were you put on this earth to do? Find that, and you'll unlock your full potential.

> The two most important days in your life are the day you are born and the day that you find out why.
> —*Mark Twain (shared by David Wood)*

Chapter 6: Craft Your Dream Career

So how do you find your passions and your purpose? Try to recall those times when you were 'in the zone' and seemed to lose track of time. Look for clues in your past.

> By the time somebody is 30 years old, you should be able to look back and see some clear patterns. 'Aha, that's why I'm doing this.' Think about when you really come alive, that's your sweet spot. It may be when you're working on ideas or are outdoors or with kids; you can start to see the patterns develop.
>
> So it's by looking inward that we get a clear sense of what that focus ought to be, what we most enjoy. A lot of people miss that. They're too quick to say, 'I hear they're hiring down at the plant,' or 'My uncle did this and he was successful, so I'll try that.' They look for external solutions—Band-Aid fixes for what they're really seeking.
>
> So I tell people, 85% of gaining the confidence to take proper direction in your career comes from looking inward. Identify what is unique about your skills and abilities, your values, dreams, and passions. Then ask the question, 'What kind of work embraces that? What kind of work embraces what I know about myself?'
> *–Dan Miller*

Kathleen Kingsbury said she was one of those "geeks that liked to balance her checkbook." She ended up being an expert combining finance and psychology. Brittney Castro shared similar interests—she liked to play with her cash register as a kid. She is now a Certified Financial Planner, running her own firm.

It all starts by reflecting, but meditating and journaling are other great ways to get to your core and uncover who you are. So many of us get overwhelmed with the task of finding our true passions, but it is important to realize a few things.

1. It takes time.

It takes many people years of reflection and learning to get to their core. JV Crum III said it took him several decades before he found his calling!

2. We are all good!

One thing that guest after guest confirmed and promoted was the fact that we are all good, and we can all become experts at something. There are many people out there who could use your expertise and interest to solve a problem of theirs.

> Know what you're good at and the position that you need to fill.
> Entrepreneurs are like superheroes; know your superpower.
> *—Matt Shoup*

We all have a superpower—it's just a matter of figuring out what that power is and using it!

3. You can adjust your course at any time.

You don't have to be stuck in one career—your passions will change and evolve over time.

4. It is never too late start finding and following your desires.

The best piece of advice that Dan Miller ever received was that it is never too late for a new beginning. Create the future that you want now instead of waiting for it to happen or regretting that you didn't do anything about it.

5. Finding your passions starts and ends with you.

> Be yourself because nobody is like you and nobody can take that away
> from you.
> *—Pat Flynn*

Don't look for outside approval—your passions are yours and yours alone. Don't be afraid to go against the grain.

Chapter 6: Craft Your Dream Career

Wealth is being on your true north. It's bringing your passions and your
purpose together. If you're not on that path, you are not living a
wealthy life.
—JV Crum III

Resolve to live with purpose and passion, and you will be on your way to
wealth.

<u>Start With Skills</u>

It's not quite as easy as simply being passionate about something and then all
of a sudden having massive success. You need to have a skill that people are
willing to pay you for.

A lot of people get hung up on passion. In order to find happiness and
true wealth, you need to have passion. But passion won't get you all the
way there. Passion is the starting point. It has to have some practical
application.
—Josh Brown

The second piece of the dream career equation—and the most important
piece for the short term—is having an in-demand skill that goes hand-in-hand
with your passion. The experts interviewed not only do something they're
passionate about, but they combine that with their unique abilities and
experiences. The best way to succeed is to use your strengths.

Focus on your strengths. The people working with their strengths are
the rock star people. They're comfortable in their own skin, great at
their jobs, enjoying life. They spend the majority of their time looking
for things and doing things that fit with them uniquely.
—Scott Barlow, career expert, co-host of Happen to Your Career podcast

Enjoying your work and doing something at which you excel are inseparable
for long-term career success. Without the skills, your company or customers
don't have much use for your passion. The trick is to combine those things so
you achieve the highest level of wealth and success.

You have got to have some skill set to match your desires or else
you're not going to be able to capitalize on the opportunities in front

of you. Too often we want to go after the shiny objects before we've built up truly valuable skills. We need a bigger focus on buckling down and becoming great at something, because what science tells us is that the more proficient you become at something, the more passionate you become about it.

—Barrett Brooks, speaker and director of member success at Fizzle.co

The Perfect Career

Think of three overlapping circles: one circle is what you're passionate about, next is what you feel you can be the best at in the world, and the third circle is the economic driver. When you connect all of those circles, the center where all three of them overlap is where you need to go.

—Josh Brown

Jim Collins' Hedgehog Concept

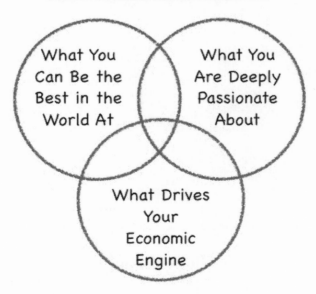

That sweet spot in the middle is where success lies. It's not really success unless it is sustainable long-term while also making both you *and* your company or customers happy.

Chapter 6: Craft Your Dream Career

The key to success that I talk about is the Triple Win. The Triple Win is when you, others, and society are all winning together. Start creating a better world in which everybody has a bigger opportunity to win.
–JV Crum III

Work doesn't have to be a bad thing. Realize that you actually can do what you're passionate about and make a lot of money doing it. It's not an *either/or* world; it is an *and* world. Find synergies and ways that you can do what you love *and* make a great living at the same time.

So many people settle for what is comfortable or 'least risky' in the short term instead of looking for a better way. The difference with the wealthy is that they never give up. Most didn't know exactly which career to choose in the beginning, and nearly all of them had multiple jobs and careers before finally arriving where they wanted to be.

The important point is that they never stopped looking. In their minds, it was never too late. They continued to search for their true passions, and they never let education or past experiences define their future.

- Ann Wilson transitioned from being an engineer in the corporate world to creating a career in the wealth industry.

- Dennis Cummins, a chiropractor for over twenty years, attended a training event and found his true calling in speaking and training.

- Tom Basso turned a chemical engineering degree into a legendary investing career.

- August Turak, already a successful entrepreneur, lived and worked among Trappist monks to help him discover the life answers he was looking for.

It doesn't matter where you are or where you've been—it only matters where you're going. The great thing is that you get to create your destination.

I learned that what we choose as a career is just a framework. You learn certain skills, but what you can do with that is up to you. You can make anything out of any career.

- 81 -

Where you start your career is very unlikely to be what you're going to do in 5-10 years. The biggest advice I can give to someone who is starting out is be flexible and open to different opportunities; explore and play! Don't let your job description define where you can add energy. There will always be a place for you to contribute and add value.
—Ann Wilson

It always goes back to the mindset—the way you're approaching and thinking about the problem. Don't think of your career as a straight line to success; think of it as a journey that zigs and zags forward. Use every experience as a stepping-stone toward your ultimate goals instead of looking for the perfect solution right from the start. Career happiness isn't as much about completion as it is about progress.

A huge part of personal freedom is being open and willing to adapt and change. As soon as we feel constricted, we start to question ourselves. Be willing to adjust course, if necessary, and follow where your interests take you. Always remember that it is your life, and you are the driver.

Vehicles for Wealth

We often look for that one job or opportunity that will make us rich, but these truths are important to repeat:

- There is no single way to build wealth. The opportunities are endless, and you can become anything you want to be.

- The best way to make money is to provide value.

This second point is key: where can you provide the most value to the world? We're all unique, and we all can make a great impact. What are the unique skills and interests that you can monetize? How can you do so?

When you think about it in terms of value and your unique skill set and interests, it opens up a world of opportunities specific to you. You now know what you want, so it is just a matter of finding the best way to get there.

The right vehicle—or career—is at the center of where your interests, skills, dream lifestyle, financial goals, desired level of security needs, and amount of growth/contribution come together, but it is also dependent on what you're willing to give up (in time and effort) to achieve that.

The wealthy experts on the podcast have found their calling in countless different fields:

- Entrepreneurship

- Network marketing

- Investing and trading

- Real estate

- Writing and speaking

- Financial planning

- Online business (e-commerce, membership sites, sales, software)

- Podcasting

- Blogging

- Coaching and training

- Freelancing

The key is that they never gave up, and they never let others' expectations hold them back. With this never-say-die attitude, each of them was eventually able to find a well-suited vehicle for their career.

Summary

A. Self-awareness is key to finding career success.

Self-awareness is one of the most important traits you can have. The wealthy know not only what they want, but also know who they are. They play to their strengths and provide as much value to the world as they can. To find their unique self and abilities, they looked to their past for clues.

> Making more money is about getting clear on who you are and what
> you can offer in the world.
> —*Brittney Castro*

B. Internal wealth comes from doing what you love.

The way to get onto your path to wealth is to start doing things that light you up inside. In life, you'll either end up doing what you love, or you'll wish you had, so you might as well go after it now!

Here are a few reasons why you should follow your passion:

- You perform better when you do work you love (and thus gain more success, make more money, and have more impact).

- There are many others who have the same passions as you do.

- You have one shot to live a passionate life. If you don't try, you'll wish you had.

It often takes time to really know and understand your passions, but it is worth analyzing them now.

> Finding your passions is different for everyone. Some people know
> exactly what they want to do. For others, it's a journey. It's something
> that doesn't happen overnight because the journey is where we become
> who we're meant to be.
> —*Jon Gordon*

You can always change. Your past and present situations are merely experiences, lessons, and relationships that will get you to where you want to go eventually. Use them as such.

C. External wealth (money) comes from combining your passions with applicable skills.

Passions are hobbies until you combine them with a practical application.

The better you are at something, the more you enjoy it. And the more you enjoy it, the more passionate you become. So some would argue that skill is even more important than passion!

Your strengths—or should I say *superpowers?*—are where the power lies. Find those, leverage them to excel in your career, and keep moving forward.

Creating the life and wealth of your dreams starts with becoming clear on what your ideal lifestyle looks like, and then combining that with your passions and skills to solve a problem. Once you have a clear picture, the vehicles you can use to apply your skills and achieve your goals are countless.

Action Items

1. Get the free sample spreadsheets, PDFs, and specific examples for all exercises from this chapter at MakeMoneyLiveWealthy.com/chapter6.

2. Describe who you are now and who you want to be.

    a. What words would you use to describe yourself right now?

    b. What qualities, characteristics and traits would you like to have?

Who You Are: Who You Want to Be:

3. "Find the things you love to do. What excites you? Write a long list. Write down why you love each thing. If that's what you love to do, then move in that direction. Focus on those passions and get a great coach who can get you through the process and help find out how you're going to make that into a living." *—Chris Locurto*

a. "What's your real passion? What really puts your soul on fire?" –*JV Crum III*

b. What is it that you desire? List everything! Are these things that you really want, or are they part of someone else's dream?

c. What would you do if money were no object? What would you do in life if you could not fail?

d. What is more important than you are, and something you could dedicate your life to?

e. Is what you're doing today something that you would start all over again tomorrow? (If not, move on from that bad decision!)

f. Lastly, what is your superpower? What made you different or unique growing up? What was one thing you did that made you stand out?

4. Find your dream career.

a. Combine your passions and skills using the hedgehog concept.

b. Brainstorm different careers. Who do you admire, and how have they combined their passions and skills in their work? Use these as ideas for how you can create your own perfect career.

<u>CHAPTER 7: MAKE MONEY</u>

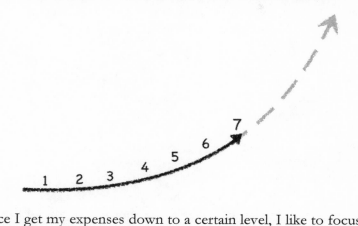

Once I get my expenses down to a certain level, I like to focus my
energy on making more money, because that is unlimited.
—Philip Taylor

Building financial wealth is a sport. The key is to create a good defense—
habits, emergency fund, savings, no debt—and then go on the offensive
attack and make some money. You can save your way to wealth, but you
shouldn't—it takes way too long. A good combination of offense and defense
will win the game every single time.

Money is important for two key reasons:

- It is a great scorecard for the value you're providing.

- It helps make achieving your goals become a reality.

Fortunately, the experts interviewed know exactly how to make a lot of
money.

The Equations of Wealth

Building wealth is simple. It's not easy, but it is simple. Make more than
you spend and invest the difference wisely. Add time to that equation,
and that is how you build wealth.
—*Rob Berger*

In essentially everything we do (especially the important areas of our lives), we
overcomplicate things. Wealth is no different. When you break it down, it is
really pretty straightforward.

Simplistically, there are three variables to the wealth equation: 1) income, 2)
expenses, and 3) what you do with the leftover money.

The better you do with each piece of the puzzle, the quicker you'll build your
wealth. I know this is easier said than done, but when you add these pieces
together and let time work its wonders, amazing things can happen for you
financially.

Ann Wilson, author of *The Wealth Chef*, shared with us her five core
foundational assets for building massive wealth:

1. "Learn how to manage your money. Pay yourself first. Understand the
difference between investing and saving.

2. Make your investments as automated as possible. Use time. Make it easy.
Get your money to work for you.

3. Get out, and stay out, of consumer debt. Debt is the biggest barrier, a
parasite to wealth.

4. Understand protection. Emergency fund, safety net in case you can't work,
insurances, and having a will and power of attorney.

5. Expand *you*—the greatest asset you have. Be clear on what knowledge you
want, who your peer groups and mentors are, how you're going to master
your mindset, and how you set goals."

Chapter 7: Make Money

Engineer, entrepreneur, and financial advisor Rob Wilson shared with us that getting rich and building wealth boils down to what he calls *The 4 P's*:

1. Potential

'If you focus on living up to your potential, you'll never have to worry about living within your means.' Frugality is limited, but the amount of money that you can make is unlimited. I would much rather people focus on how they can make more money and how can they utilize their skills to their maximum potential than try to figure out how to cut things out of their budget. Be the very best and understand at a very deep level what your superpower. Leverage that to make money.

2. Product

Everybody has a product to sell, but most people unfortunately sell only their time. Again, there's a cap to that. There are so many hours in a day, and you can't create more. If you truly want to build wealth, you have to have a product to sell that can be sold whether you're there or not, whether you're awake or you're asleep, whether you're in a golf course or in the office. The product needs to be out there making money for you. I think a lot of people can start their wealth-building strategy by creating products around whatever their expertise is.

3. People

It can't always be about your product—you need to have other people out there selling it for you. Even if you're a one-person business, you need a virtual assistant or someone to take non-value-added activity away from you so you can focus on what it is that you do best.

4. Property

Once you have maximized your potential, created a product, and have people selling for you, then you invest the incoming cash. Investments start to generate revenue and income for you on an ongoing basis. That's how you create true financial independence—when your assets are paying your expenses.

Another important factor in becoming rich is taking care of different time frames—now, in the near future, and over the long term. Patrick Bet-David, a financial services entrepreneur, shared some great advice on how you should position yourself financially:

> The simplest way to think about it is to look at everything with your finances as three buckets you've got to fill up:
>
> 1) Short term: 0-12 months
>
> 2) Midterm: 1-10 years
>
> 3) Long term: 10 years plus
>
> Find out which of those buckets is full and which needs a lot of help. Most of the time, you start off with step number 1. How much cash do you have set aside?
>
> Then, what do you have in your midterm bucket? What events may be taking place in your life in the next 1-10 years that you need to start saving money for?
>
> Longer term, you're talking about retirement. One of the smartest things one could do is get bucket number 3 squared away in your 20s, but this is rarely done. Most think, "Oh, retirement's so far away; I'll just do it later on." But you've got to get that in place in your 20s.
>
> In a nutshell, if you can write those three buckets down—short term, midterm, long term—and you really gauge yourself and rank yourself on how well you're doing on each one, and you try to improve in that area, eventually things should work out for you.
> *—Patrick Bet-David*

Things should work out *very, very well* for you, in fact. Financial security at its finest is taking care of the past (debt), present (cash), and future (year one thru retirement). Cover those, and you are rich, indeed.

At the end of the day, the formula is quite simple—keep it that way.

Chapter 7: Make Money

Money doesn't have to be complicated. When I realized that, my wealth expanded both in terms of life experiences and money. My money expanded because I just let it be simple, straightforward, and I trusted that process with time and focus.

—Ann Wilson

Types of Income

There's no secret. You can build wealth in an infinite number of ways.
—Rob Berger

There are countless ways to make more money, but the way you go about making that money is very important. There are three types of income:

1. Working Income

2. Residual Income

3. Passive Income

These three types of income highlight the three ways you can earn money:

1. Do work once; get paid once.

2. Do work once; get paid multiple times.

3. Do no work, but still get paid.

The options get better and better, yet most are only familiar with working income.

Let's break these down in more detail.

1. Working Income

This is, of course, the income that you get from working. Think corporate jobs, teachers, medical personnel, fast food workers, or anybody else who gets paid on an hourly or salaried basis.

The bad part about working income is that your earnings are capped. If you want to make more money, you have to work more hours or negotiate a higher wage. There are only so many hours in a day, so the upside is limited.

Make Money, Live Wealthy

Many often get into the situation of working more and more hours for a similar salary (after inflation), thus working themselves into a pay cut.

But before you start thinking, 'I can't get rich from working this job,' think again. It may not be the best way to build massive wealth, but it is definitely possible.

> There's nothing wrong with being an employee who works for a large company, building a career serving a large and established entity. People should have a very strong self-check to make sure that they are doing what they would feel most comfortable and most passionate about.
> *–Erez Katz*

Ann Wilson was an engineer in the corporate world for much of her career. She then ventured off on her own, much like many of the other expert guests.

> Just because you're working in a corporate, salaried environment doesn't mean you can't get rich. It's not what you earn, but what you do with the money that really counts.
> *–Ann Wilson*

That is important—it's not how much you make, but how much you keep and what you do with the money that really counts!

Tom Basso managed people's money for a long time at his own firm, but when he reflected on his career, he would think about potentially staying on as an engineer and building up his own fund.

> I would give serious consideration to making more as an engineer, saving more, investing more, managing my own money ,and trading my way right into retirement. I considered skipping the money management game.
> *–Tom Basso*

For many people, working income is the majority, if not all, of the income. If you have plans to keep working income as your main income stream, then you'll want to focus on maximizing your salary and building the right practices around saving and investing so that you can still amass the riches you desire.

Chapter 7: Make Money

2. Residual Income

The second type of income you can make is called residual income.

Residual income is money earned over and over again from work you do one time.

The great thing about residual income is not only do you get paid multiple times for your efforts, but it can be scaled and thus grow exponentially (versus working income typically being linear). Once you stop working, you can still be paid for your efforts. When you trade your time for money, this isn't the case.

The main drawbacks are that it still requires work up front to make residual income, and you don't get the instant gratification that a paycheck provides. It is a delayed, but powerful income stream that can be scaled.

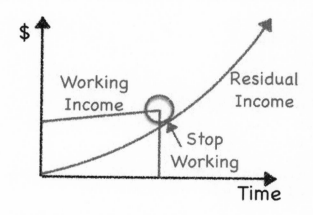

Examples of residual income are network marketing, investing, online information products or software, books or music, and so on.

3. Passive Income

Passive income and residual income are very closely related, and they are often discussed (mistakenly) as the same thing. However, passive income is the best of all.

Make Money, Live Wealthy

*Passive income is income in which you've set up some sort of a system
to receive that income whether you're working or not.*
—Kate Northrup

Examples of passive income may include investing (stock market, real estate, small businesses), network marketing, online businesses (E-commerce, membership subscriptions, affiliate marketing, software), and other avenues that don't require your active involvement.

Regardless of the method, approaching your wealth in ways that give you the best return on your time and effort will result in much higher income in the long run.

Passive income isn't easy to get at first. It often takes some time, but primarily comes through two avenues:

1. Putting your money to work for you (i.e. stock market, real estate investments, dividends, T-Bills, bonds).

2. Putting your business to work for you (i.e. real estate rentals, online business, affiliate sales, network marketing).

Many of the wealthy start by building a residual income stream, grow that, and then turn it into a passive income source. They then continue to put those earnings to work for them, further growing their funds. It is a cycle that grows and grows and adds up quickly.

*You need to find a vehicle that creates residual income that you can
turn into passive income.*
—David Wood

Once you create enough passive income, you're headed towards financial freedom.

Chapter 7: Make Money

	Non-Wealthy	Wealthy
Income Focus	Working income— trade time for money.	Passive income—How do I get paid multiple times for my efforts? How do I get paid for as little work as possible?
How to get more money	Work more hours or get another job.	Scale passive/residual income vehicles
Goal	Higher salary	Financial Freedom

Financial Freedom

Financial freedom is when your passive or residual income exceeds your living expenses.
—Kate Northrup

This means that you can stop working but still go on living your life.

Wealth is the ability to live and prosper in life. You can quit your job, walk away, and continue your lifestyle because of the passive income that you have.
—Anton Ivanov

The traditional way to retire is to work for a long time, save, and build up enough of a fund so that you can retire at the age of 65 (if you're lucky). However, there is a much, much better way.

The better way is to create financial freedom. It doesn't matter what specific vehicle you use—the goal is to do the least amount of work in order to have the freedom and life that you desire.

We're all going to spend a large part of our life working, so we might as well enjoy what we do and work smart so we can be paid numerous times for our efforts.

The easy route in the short term, however, is the instant satisfaction you receive in a paycheck. When you get used to money coming in on a regular basis, it's difficult to leave it for something else. Michael Kawula calls it "the addiction to the paycheck."

But it's not only the financial aspect of passive/residual income that is appealing. It's really about the time and the freedom that we're after. Instead of waiting until they were 65 to be able to retire, many of the expert guests found financial freedom in their 20s by focusing on residual and passive income early in their careers.

> Part of the reason I focus on passive income is a lifestyle thing. I don't like to have to do anything on one certain day. I want to set up my life in a way that if I want to travel today, I can do that. If I just want to take the day off and be with friends and family, I can do that.
>
> Another thing for me is that I have the worst form of entrepreneurial ADD. There's always something I want to work on. A lot of times I set up a business and automate it, and then I can go work on whatever else is grabbing my attention. It maybe is not the most profitable strategy, but I prefer to set up niche businesses, automate them, and then go work on another business. It is kind of rinse and repeat. This has worked well for me.
> —Billy Murphy

This is why it is key to figure out your lifestyle goal first. From there, you can start to work toward the type of career and income streams that will help get you that lifestyle.

Money Secrets of the Rich

There's no one secret formula on how to make money, but there are tons of tips that the wealthy use to get rich.

First of all, do you know what the biggest expense that you will likely have in your lifetime is?

It is not your mortgage or that yacht you're going to buy—it's taxes. As a result, the wealthy understand how to minimize the amount of taxes they pay.

Chapter 7: Make Money

Even a small percentage difference on how much you pay in taxes on your income and investments can have a huge impact over time.

> Every time you make sure Uncle Sam can't get your money, you are making money just by virtue of not being taxed.
> —*Laurie Itkin, financial advisor, author, The Options Lady*

So what do the wealthy do about taxes? They have a business entity that they use to build their wealth (Chapter 8), and they also invest in a way that takes advantage of the options available to them (Chapter 9). Most people handle their taxes blindly, but if you want to model yourself after the wealthy, you must be cognizant of the tax implications and take advantage of the opportunities available to you.

In addition, something repeated countless times was the value in having multiple sources of income. This is especially true for those looking to build wealth in a corporate or salaried career.

> Companies are laying off employees every day. Nobody wants to invest in a business that has one customer. If you have only one stream of income, that's something that can go away tomorrow.
> —*Rob Wilson*

In addition to multiple streams, you will want to maximize your salary. The way to do that is to give massive value, and then show your employer that value.

> There's no way you're going to be in a position to ask for more money unless you are providing more. Ask yourself the question, 'Am I kicking tail at my job?' Establish what the expectations are and exceed those expectations on a weekly basis, but also know what you're worth in the marketplace. From the employer's perspective, it is all about return on investment. Show what they're going to get in return.
> —*Scott Barlow*

The popular way used to be to work for a large, established company and stay there your entire career. That may not be the case in today's environment. Patrick Bet-David was young and eager to make a lot of money, so he walked into a very wealthy man's office and asked him for advice.

Make Money, Live Wealthy

He said, "Do you want to become wealthy?" *Yes.* "No, do you *really*
want to become wealthy? Rule #1: never, ever, ever work for a sexy,
established company. Big, sexy, established companies are sexy and
established because a group of people helped that company become
sexy and established and now those people are wealthy. Go to a small
company and help it become sexy and established. Be a voice, be a
leader, be an adviser, and you will become wealthy. No wealthy person
is impressed by you working for a big company. Start with somebody's
small business and make something big out of it. Make a name for
yourself, and wealth should be right around the corner for you."
—Patrick Bet-David

Entrepreneurship—or joining a startup or small growing business—can be
the best way to create wealth for yourself. Richard Wilson shared that the best
return on his money he can get is by investing in his own business. Second to
that, investing in other small businesses can provide great returns. It goes
back to networking and taking action to see these opportunities, which
anybody can do.

Another important thing to note is how money moves and flows. The best
place for making money in the last few years may not be the best place to
make money in the future. Different markets go through cycles, and the best
investors I know are those who are able to move their money into different
vehicles to take advantage of big trends.

The key is to think differently and strategically, but it still all starts with one
thing—the mindset. You may be concerned about this month's bills instead
of how to make $100 million, but the most important secret you can learn
about money is the magic of dreaming and believing big!

The thing about wealth and finances is that most of us limit
ourselves. The magic of thinking big is the secret to finances,
definitely.
—Trevor Blake, successful entrepreneur, New York Times bestselling author of
Three Simple Steps

Not only do you need to be ambitious, but you absolutely must think about
how you can best help other people. If you have this focus, the money will
show up.

Chapter 7: Make Money

The key to making money, according to Dan Miller, is to create amazing relationships.

> I focus on creating amazing relationships, doing the things I really love, and serving other people well. And you know what? Money just shows up, even in unexpected ways.

> What can I do to increase my service to my customers? Answer that question in new and better ways, and profit will take care of itself.

> No man can become rich without enriching others.
> —*Dan Miller*

In the long run, the amount of money you earn is a scorecard for the impact and value you provide to society.

> You need to have money on your mind, but impact drives income— not the other way around. You have to get out there and have more impact and influence; that's when the income starts coming in.

> You get paid for bringing value to a marketplace, and if you're not very valuable, you don't make much money. You're going to be paid exactly what you're worth or what you expect you're worthy of.

> You have to figure out how to help people. If you focus on impact and influence instead of income, it causes you to be more valuable. It gets you thinking how to help others instead of how to help yourself.
> —*Peter Voogd*

Another key is to keep your earnings uncapped. With an hourly wage, you're limited by the hours you can spend working. With a salary, you don't have much upside. What you want to find are ways that you can work with a very high ceiling.

Steve Burns prefers investing because the upside is unlimited. Peter Voogd was excited about a direct sales job he got because it was finally a chance for him to get paid based on his potential instead of what the company thought he was worth. He had more control over his earnings, which is exactly what you want.

Make Money, Live Wealthy

Another critical component of becoming rich is taking risk, but the wealthy view what risk really is in a completely different manner. Billy Murphy said that the biggest thing he learned from being a professional poker player was how to evaluate the risks he should and should not take.

Most people view risk as anything where you're going to take a chance at something and lose money. They think, *Lets make whatever decision is going to lose me the least amount of money.* Instead, you want to be making decisions that will make you the most money.

For a poker player, that becomes second nature. Every decision you make in poker is called EV, or expected value. You want every decision to be the most profitable decision. A lot of people are results oriented, but as a poker player, you don't care whether you win or lose. What's important is, did I make the right decision? Did I make the most profitable decision? Did it make me more money over the long term?

I feel like almost everybody struggles with that. When you're playing poker, you have to think like that or you'll never make any money. It translates into business really well because a lot of people want to start a business, but it seems risky. 'I could lose all my money,' so you're going to stay in your job, keep your money in the bank, and not do anything.

Let's say that somebody has a goal of having $10K per month passively. With them avoiding any possible risks, they're basically guaranteeing themselves that they will never hit their goal. However, if they started taking EV decisions, they could calculate that maybe the winner will lose a couple of times, but over the long run, they're going to hit their goal.

Let's say somebody has a job and makes $50K a year. His EV—what he's going to make in that job each year—is $50K. Now he considers starting a business. If this business goes really well, what can he expect it to do? Then he calculates another return for the business doing fairly well. Then he considers the worst-case scenario: losing his entire investment. So he takes the likelihood of each of those three scenarios and combines the numbers to calculate

Chapter 7: Make Money

his EV in that business. He may very well determine that the job is
actually way riskier than trying the business.

You could lose money in the business; but by making the negative
EV decision and staying on the job, you're basically guaranteeing
that you lose money long term. A lot of people think very short
term, but avoiding risk is often riskier than taking chances.
–Billy Murphy

There is an opportunity cost that may be far more risky than doing nothing,
so be sure to objectively view how 'risky' things really are. This is a key
differentiator between the rich and the poor. It's not that the rich take more
or less risk—it is that they better understand the odds and act accordingly.

All it takes is one leap of faith, one opportunity—and the rest could be
history.

Marcus Sheridan shared the story of the turning point in his life. Too broke to
take a cab home from the airport and deep into the Great Recession, he
stepped outside his comfort zone and took a chance. He entered the office of
the woman running a conference he was attending and said, 'I'm the best
speaker you've never heard' (with a smile on his face). Eventually, she gave
him his chance.

Knowing that this was his big shot, he put further pressure on himself by
inviting the biggest names he could find at the conference to come see his
talk. They attended, and he gave the best presentation of his life. From there,
he went on to get more and more speaking gigs, and now he makes as much
as $15,000 for a single speech. Let's just say he no longer worries about
money. The lesson is—one door often opens the opportunities for many
others . . . *if* you take advantage of them.

Another big fear is that making money is really hard to do. Justin Williams,
however, said that learning *how* to make the money is ten times harder than
actually making the money. Once you learn how, it is all about executing.

By reading this book, you are much further along the path toward making a
lot of money than you initially believed. By learning about selflessness, the

mindset, multiple streams of income, and these other 'secrets' shared by the experts, you are well on your way. Now take action!

There are only seven days in a week, and *someday* is not one of them.
—*Sean Ogle*

Habits of the Wealthy

Eighty-five percent of everything we do on any given day are the same habits and faults that we did the day before.
—*Erlend Bakke*

Your habits create who you are—and they also create who you aren't.

We live in a world of instant gratification. It is really about understanding that the things we do today, like the habits that we have today, are manifested in the future.
—*Erlend Bakke*

Changing your habits is a huge challenge, but in order to get where you want to go, it is absolutely essential to remove or minimize the damaging habits from your life.

Changing habits is one of the most difficult things we can do as human beings. Habits are so engrained in who we are as people. It's a slow process.

I'm all about consistency and doing things over time because I know that will make everything I want in my life happen. The compound effect is the more I do the productive habits, the better the results are over time.
—*Erlend Bakke*

Unsurprisingly, the wealthy have habits that help differentiate them from the pack. Hal Elrod started to really turn his life around when he incorporated personal development into his daily routine. He did some research and found the six best methods to practice:

Chapter 7: Make Money

1) Meditation

2) Affirmation

3) Visualization

4) Exercise

5) Reading

6) Journaling

Hal now does a combination of these practices daily for an hour. He calls it "personal development on steroids." Erlend Bakke was working morning, noon, and night, seven days a week, trying to build a business and get rich. The stress added up, and he had a massive anxiety attack. After that, he finally took the mindset and balance advice seriously and incorporated new and different habits that helped him become much more effective and far less stressed.

> I started sitting for 10 minutes in a chair every single day just focusing on the things that I wanted to attract into my life. It wasn't like from one day to the next, but it got easier and easier. I also do 20 minutes of meditation in the morning, journal in the evening, and power walk.
> —Erlend Bakke

From there, his business, health, and life took off. Now he has extraordinary businesses operating without much interaction from him, and he's living his dream life.

His story is important because the most important habits that you develop may affect your health. If you don't have health, relationships, meaning, and all of the other things that the experts talk about, what good is money?

> True wealth to me means you have rich loving relationships and vibrant physical health. I think people who are scrambling so much after a dollar—they're 50 pounds overweight with headaches, backaches, and compromised health. Why are they accumulating money? What's it going to mean when they don't have the physical strength to enjoy it?
> —Dan Miller

Make Money, Live Wealthy

Pat Flynn shared the story of some advice he heard from billionaire Richard Branson. Somebody asked the serial entrepreneur how he gets so much done, and he said his number one productivity tip is exercise.

> He knows that staying fit is just a trickle down effect into everything else that you do. So, if there is one thing I would recommend for anybody to become more productive, it is to eat better and get some exercise.
> *—Pat Flynn*

The sum of your habits, both good and bad, affects the position you are in at any point in your life—whether it be health, wealth, or anything else.

Change your habits, and you change your life.

Summary

A. Wealth is simple but not always easy.

The way to achieve something big is by breaking it down into smaller parts. Your money is no different. There are only three pieces to the wealth equation but all are vital—control your money, make more money, and grow your money. Build that defense (foundation, habits, expenses) and then go on the offensive attack and make unlimited money!

> There are two sides to the money equation—money in and money out. It's not just about chasing the more money side of the equation, but increasing the gap between the two.
> *—Matt Shoup*

B. Financial freedom is the ultimate money goal.

> Wealth, in the financial perspective, is when cash flow exceeds expenses.
> *—Todd Tresidder*

Most people only know of, and focus on, working income. They trade time for money. The problem with that is if they want more money, they need to work more hours. However, the wealthy view things differently. They're always looking at ways they can earn money numerous times for their efforts.

Chapter 7: Make Money

Passive income is all about the fact that you don't have to trade your time directly for money. You can build businesses that take advantage of systems of automation, and are able to have transactions and growth without requiring your time.

—Pat Flynn

Type of Income	Examples	Advantages	Disadvantages
Working Income	Hourly wage or salaried employees	Consistent, predictable (short term).	Trading time for money; when you stop working, you stop getting paid.
Residual Income	Book, network marketing, online business, investing	Get paid multiple times for doing work once (without any additional effort).	Requires up front work to set up vehicle to get paid over and over again, but may not get immediate satisfaction of making money. Not guaranteed.
Passive Income	Can be investing, real estate, network marketing, affiliate marketing, online business	Little or no work required to get paid. Continues on, even while you sleep. Creates financial and time freedom.	Doesn't happen overnight. You either need to turn residual income into passive income, or have money work for you.

You're going to spend many hours of your life working, so you might as well spend a good portion of it focused on something that will pay you multiple times for working once. The trick is to work smarter, not harder, and focusing on residual and passive income is doing just that.

Chapter 7: Make Money

C. The way to riches is having your money situation covered for multiple time frames.

Patrick Bet-David identified the three buckets: 0-12 months, 1-10 years, and longer term (retirement).

If you have each of these situations covered, then you are rich indeed.

D. The rich do it differently.

They think differently, and their strategies are different. A few tricks are to:

- Think big, and believe in that vision!

- Have multiple streams of income. (This is a great idea whether you work for yourself or not.)

- Focus on impact and influence because these things drive income.

- The best place for your money may move from one vehicle to another over time. The wealthy have the network and knowledge to be able to capitalize on these trends.

E. Your habits create who you are.

> I encourage everybody to start thinking long term. What kind of habits
> do you need in your life on a consistent basis to get the returns you
> want in five years? What are you willing to do for a long period of time?
> We have daily, weekly, monthly, and yearly habits. Being clear on those
> is very important.
> —*Erlend Bakke*

Eighty-five percent of what we do on any day is made up of habits identical to those of the previous day. Changing our habits takes effort and repetition, but it is absolutely necessary if you want to get different—and better—results.

The wealthy do a number of things on a regular basis that help them excel. The most commonly shared practices are meditation, affirmation, visualization, exercise, reading, and journaling. These are all essential to creating the mindset, clarity, and health that we all desire.

<u>Action Items</u>

1. Get the resources and free guides at MakeMoneyLiveWealthy.com/chapter7, including great daily habits and a guide on passive and residual income.

2. "Look at the equation: money in, money out. What does your money-in look like? What are your expenses? If you keep doing what you're doing right now, where is that going to end you up? If it's not going to take you where you want to be, you have to change something." *–Matt Shoup*

- This is important. Are you headed to where you want to go? If not, you need to take control and take yourself to the next level.

3. Look back at your lifestyle goal—figure out what type(s) of income you need to help get you to that goal as quickly as possible and some potential additional income streams that could potentially grow your worth. This is a key part of your wealth plan.

- Additional income streams are a great way to use your skills and passions and also a great means by which to test out a new career before making the leap from your one.

4. Incorporate a daily ritual in your life which includes one of the recommended habits. Start small and work your way up from there. Take care of your health—first and foremost. Without it, nothing else matters. Eat right and exercise daily. The result will be more money and increased happiness.

"Physical and financial health are both very important. If you don't have physical health, you can't do anything. If you don't have financial health, you can't do very much, either." *–Tom Basso*

CHAPTER 8: ENTREPRENEURIAL SUCCESS

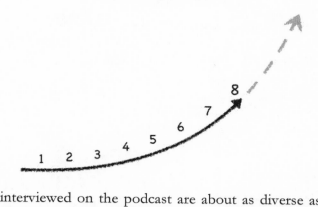

The experts interviewed on the podcast are about as diverse as you can get, but each and every guest shares one major commonality—they are all entrepreneurs.

Regardless of whether or not you decide to become an entrepreneur yourself, the business lessons and the mentality you develop from thinking like an entrepreneur will pay massive dividends in your career. Either way, you must become the CEO of You!

Why Entrepreneurship

It is no surprise that entrepreneurship is the vehicle of choice for the wealthy—there is no better way to get both the earnings and the freedom that everyone dreams of. Some of the many benefits of starting your own business are:

- The amount you can earn is unlimited, and the options are endless.

- "Building a business is the best for long-term financial freedom. Regular working income is linear, but building a business has the potential for exponential growth." –*Nick Loper, Founder of Side Hustle Nation blog and podcast*

- "There's the passive nature of it as well. It's no longer a trading time for dollars situation. If you're an entrepreneur, you can leverage it up and figure out a way to scale it to where it is bringing in money on its own." *—Philip Taylor*

- You can do anything you want. You make the decisions. Since it's your own business, it can be anything you'd like. You can do what you're passionate about (and delegate what you're not).

- In addition, you can really make a positive impact on the world! "Entrepreneurship is factored into making lives better—not just for ourselves but also for those around us." *—Jason Vitug*

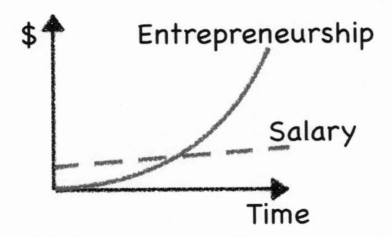

The entrepreneurship success stories that the experts shared are countless and inspiring.

- Shortly after being fired, Matt Shoup started a business. He began that journey by getting kicked out of the bank with only $100, but within a few years, he turned that into a multi-million-dollar painting business.

- Trevor Blake didn't start his first business until his 40s, but in a short period of time he has sold two businesses for over $100 million each.

Chapter 8: Entrepreneurial Success

- Peter Voogd didn't want to be told how much he was worth, so he started his own business and created his first six-figure earnings in six months.

- David Wood was told that he was 'the worst student in 37 years of teaching' and that he'd end up in jail or on the streets. Yet he found out that he had a choice, and he then made the decision to become wealthy, found the vehicles that worked for him, and now has made millions of dollars many times over. All of this when his turning point didn't come until he was 42 years old!

It doesn't matter where you start out, what your education is, who you know right now, or what your age is—you can succeed as an entrepreneur. You just have to take the right actions and fail forward.

The Challenge

I say to people looking to develop a company, 'Sometimes it's going to feel like you're in the gym. It's going to hurt, but often you'll feel good at the end.'
—*Mike Faith*

As attractive as entrepreneurship sounds, there are risks. Being in complete control of your destiny is a bit scary at first for most, and it is that way for a reason—many people fail.

Succeeding in your own business takes time and (gasp!) work.

Justin Williams started a business and quickly found himself $120,000 in debt. So he had to cut ties and basically start over. Fortunately, he has not only survived, but has thrived since that setback. The biggest lesson he learned from this experience was simply, "Business is hard."

You have to hustle and grind.

Make Money, Live Wealthy

> I meet a lot of wannabe entrepreneurs. They don't realize what you
> have to sacrifice to start a brand-new business: the time commitment,
> the emotional ups and downs. It is not easy; it is not for the faint of
> heart.
> *—Erez Katz*

The sacrifices are necessary, but the rewards make it worth it. If you learn the basics, are smart about your approach, and are willing to put in the time and effort up front, you can most definitely succeed as an entrepreneur.

<u>Is It For You?</u>

One thing most people don't consider is the fact that anything involves risk. People think that entrepreneurship is risky, but what is even more risky is not taking control of your future and putting it in the hands of someone else.

> Harvey McKay released a study showing that 90% of young
> professionals have a chance of being fired within the next 10 years.
> That's more risky than trying out a dream or passion.
> *—Michael Kawula*

If you're going to risk something, you might as well take a risk at something you enjoy, right?

If your dreams are big—which they absolutely should be—you'll have to make some sacrifices and take some risks. But remember, the biggest risk is in not taking any risk at all.

> You have to figure out two things:
> 1) What you want and how wealthy you want to become.
> 2) What you're willing to give up to get what you want.
> *—Peter Voogd*

If all of this excites you, then you are fit to be an entrepreneur. If not, maybe your focus should be on advancing your career and looking to maximize additional income streams (i.e. investing).

The key is to go back to your goals. What type of life do you want? What type of lifestyle do you want? What type of income does that require? How can you best combine your passions and skills to give you the money and lifestyle that you desire?

Just remember the big picture. It is all about freedom—financial freedom, time freedom, and the freedom to choose. For many, entrepreneurship is the answer. For others, it isn't, and that is perfectly okay.

How to Get Started

The only way to become an entrepreneur is to be an entrepreneur, and the only way to be an entrepreneur is to start.
—Jason Vitug

So you may be excited about potentially becoming an entrepreneur, but the question now is, "Where do I start?"

The experts' answer to this question was very consistent: find a problem and solve it.

The definition of an entrepreneur is someone who solves people's problems for a profit.
—David Wood

So how do you find a problem you can solve? The options are endless. Start with a challenge that you or someone else has. What is something that you complain about or wish there was a solution for?

Most successful entrepreneurs become successful because they get pissed off at something. Find your motivation by looking for things you want to improve or gaps in the market that you want to fill.
—Trevor Blake

Often we find these 'gaps' in our current careers or in areas where we spend a lot of time. This is where you want to start because that is your area of expertise, and you have familiarity with the problem. It is much more difficult to create something totally unrelated to your experiences.

> Try to emulate others before you innovate. Learn what is known in the industry before you try to come out with something brand new.
> —*Richard Wilson*

There are always areas for improvement in any field or industry; you just have to dive deep into them to find the gaps and then fill them.

Keep your eyes open and try to find those inefficiencies in your everyday work and life. The best way to become an entrepreneur is to start to think like one. Start to notice challenges or bottlenecks in a process and ask lots of questions. The potential for new ideas is infinite.

Richard Wilson went through several different roles in a field in which he was interested. He was looking for more information about family hedge fund offices, yet he couldn't find any resources. So he created them himself. He not only started the number one website educating people on the topic, but he also created his own certification program to help further increase his credibility. Now he represents the go-to resource in the niche.

Erez Katz put it well when he said, "Don't think about the *idea*. Think about the *need* you're going to fulfill." Do this and you're well on your way to becoming a successful entrepreneur.

The Market Matters

> Think about how can you create something in a strong and growing market and ride the wave.
> —*Tim Harrington, president of BattleFin (investing tournaments)*

The problem that you'll be solving is key, but it helps immensely if you're in the right market. This will make everything much easier, but it's not good enough to just be in the right market. The wealthy podcast guests strongly suggested that you go even further and create an uncontested market space.

The way you do this is by creating an entirely new market altogether *or* by niching down until you're the best in your specific market. The key is to separate yourself and be unique.

Chapter 8: Entrepreneurial Success

Make sure not to go too broad. Find a more specific niche so you can progress faster. Define the area of business within your niche where you're only competing with a few people. If you're just generic, how are you ever going to stand out as the person who should be paid more or as the one with the most expertise?
— *Richard Wilson*

Niching down and targeting the right audience is crucial. But how do you do that? Mike Michalowicz says to start at a high level and work your way down.

When you're a brand new start-up, you don't know what you don't know. If you try to niche down, most of the time you pick the wrong niche.

In the very beginning of a business, you need to pick someone to start marketing to. Start with the people like you—or people like you used to be —because you know how to communicate with them. Keep your ears wide open because it may not be them who resonate with your message.
—Mike Michalowicz

Mike thought that the audience for his first book was male college grads. He pushed and pushed into this market until he realized that his target market was actually middle-aged women. As soon as he realized that, his book took off to amazing levels.

You have to start broad, but you have to see what resonates with customers. It's easy to determine this: they are the ones reaching out to you or buying repeatedly from you. You need to measure their actions and not their words. Once you know who's resonating with you, focus your efforts on collecting them.
—Mike Michalowicz

<u>Complete Awareness</u>

Entrepreneurship may seem like a great option, but as with any career, it only works great long term if it is aligned with who you are, what your interests are, and what you bring to the world. Having self-awareness and clarity on these things is of the utmost importance for a successful career.

> When setting up a business, know what the proposition is. What solution are you bringing? What problem are you going to resolve?
> —*John Murphy*

Figure out what August Turak calls 'the business of the business', and you'll be in good shape.

> You really need to know how your business operates—the ins and outs, how business flows from start to finish—and especially know what you're good at. Entrepreneurs are like superheroes.
> —*Matt Shoup*

Know what your superpower is—and use it. Leverage your skills and find people to help in areas where you are weak.

Entrepreneurship, much like any worthwhile endeavor, is going to entail some tough times. To be able to weather those lows, you need to keep an eye on the big picture. Why are you doing what you're doing? Why should you sacrifice and push through this challenge? Clarifying the answers to these questions early will pay big dividends later on.

You not only need to have a strong purpose for doing what you do, but you should also be interested and skilled in the market.

> Once your business has started, you're going to end up establishing yourself as an expert in that domain. Your business has to be that authoritative voice in that domain, and if you're not really natural in that field, you're going to seem like a fraud. People will see right through it.
> —*Alex Genadinik, serial entrepreneur, top app developer*

Chapter 8: Entrepreneurial Success

Combine passion, purpose, and perseverance with a problem solved, and you have the makings for success with entrepreneurship.

Give, Give, Give

I think the greatest thing, whatever you do, is to create value for people. Put people first, not money. If you help other people get what they want, you'll always get what you want.
—David Wood

Not only do you need to know what value you provide, but you need to give a lot of it. If you want to *get*, you must first *give*.

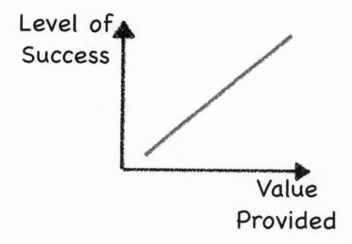

The level of success you achieve directly correlates with the value you provide. Customers will come because you offer a solution and build their trust. The best way to build that trust is to provide something of value first.

When you're giving something of value, people stand in line and say, 'I want to be part of that.' I based my business model on giving away 95% of everything that we do. We've done pretty well with the remaining 5%.
—Dan Miller

Make Money, Live Wealthy

This outward focus is one of the most important elements of success in any area of life. The more you give, the more you get. If you have a great purpose and create a ton of value, you will have no choice but to be extremely successful.

August Turak shared some lessons that he learned firsthand living and working amongst the Trappist monks. These monks are extremely mission-oriented and are thus focused on service and selflessness. The result of this is that they're very good at it, and this has lead to timeless business success for them—1500 years and counting.

> Making money is about 5 steps down the line from the mission. The less I think about money, the more money I make. Selflessness is the key.
> —*August Turak*

Take Massive Action

> You need to take that vision, put it down on paper, and just do it. I see a lot of entrepreneurs who get tied up from getting started. It's like having kids; you're never going to be 100% ready or secure, but you have to just pull the trigger.
> —*Matt Shoup*

You don't need to know everything, and that's okay because you never will! As Jason Vitug said, you aren't an entrepreneur unless you start.

> A great piece of advice is to allow it to be an imperfect action because if you wait for everything to be aligned, you will be waiting your entire life.
> —*Ann Wilson*

One of the best ways to get over the fear of entrepreneurship and reduce the risk is to start small. The majority of the experts didn't move from one job straight into entrepreneurship on their own. They bridged their career and most often started something on the side, found out some things that they liked and didn't like, and built that 'side-hustle' until they were confident that this new path was absolutely right for them.

Chapter 8: Entrepreneurial Success

If your goal is entrepreneurship of any form, start heading there now. That is when you'll really learn. You don't have to go all-in right away, but use your current position to learn and progress toward where you want to go.

> I used my corporate experiences as stepping stones to becoming my own boss someday. I realized I needed to learn financials, so I went down that track. I began to travel a lot and found a common problem, so I'm solving that now.
> —*Jason Vitug*

The important thing is that you're moving forward, taking action, and heading to where you ultimately want to go. The action is more important than the plan at this point, and no business plan is necessary.

> A business plan is a static document. If you can predict the revenue for a company that doesn't exist yet in two years, that means you can predict the stock market. The numbers are nonsense; no one can predict the numbers. Business plans just say that you've got one shot, and that's why 99% of business plans sit on the shelf.
> —*Mike Michalowicz*

What you *do* need to launch a business, per Mike, are what he calls *the last three sheets* from his book, *The Toilet Paper Entrepreneur*:

1.) Vision statement (prosperity plan).

- This defines where you want to head.

2.) Tacking (a strategy of adjusting your course as you go).

- You don't go directly to where you're headed; you leverage the current environment. You can't get there in a straight line. What will you do next quarter that will get you as close to your prosperity plan as possible?

3.) Daily metrics (the heartbeat of your company).

- Pick the critical number that tells you how healthy your business is at any moment and monitor it on a daily basis. When you monitor on a daily basis, if there's a problem, you can adjust it. If things are good, you keep tacking along until you reach the end of the 90 days, realign, and push forward again.

So, you have to define where you want to go, tack and adjust on a regular basis (Mike suggests every 90 days), and use the most critical numbers as your guide. This plan will keep you moving forward, focused yet flexible. But the key is to get into action at some point—just start.

> If you have a dream or a goal, don't wait ten years and look back and say, *I wish I could have*. Just do it; take action today.
> —*Michael Kawula*

Go Pro

The turning point toward massive success in entrepreneurship is when you decide to 'go pro.'

Going pro is the idea of turning a hobby into a business and going all-in. It is the mindset that you will not fail and you're going to be committed to your success as an entrepreneur. When you decide to do that, you are unstoppable.

Many successful entrepreneurs have a certain level of internal confidence (often external, as well) because it is absolutely necessary. You need that inner belief to be able to get over the inevitable fears that will surface in the process.

> Allowing yourself to raise that level of certainty and eliminating self-doubt is important to any young entrepreneur—an essential part of embracing that journey.
> —*Larry Stevens*

Richard Wilson said that if he had done anything differently, he would have listened to himself and gone forward more confidently. Steve Burns said, 'You have to have faith in yourself and the right psychology. Otherwise, you will not make it.'

The shift to going pro makes you start to think of everything in terms of a business. Where can my time be best spent for the bottom line? What things can I systemize and scale? What things can I delegate? Your time is the equivalent of money or freedom. Spend it wisely.

> Moving from a hobby to a business requires a mind shift. At first, I worked hard, not smart. Then I started figuring out things to leverage—consultants, freelancers, people who can help me do the things for my business that I couldn't do myself. I pay them to help me do the special things to make my business unique or more successful.
> *—Philip Taylor*

Successful entrepreneurs not only work hard, they work smart. They build a team of like-minded people who are, as Peter Voogd says, "playing the game at a higher level."

> Find partners who can complement your skill sets. Build a solid team. Bring on extremely talented and passionate employees who share your vision.
> *—Erez Katz*

JV Crum III and others said that their biggest mistake early on was being a 'solopreneur' and trying to do it all themselves. It is hard to do it alone, so don't. Successful entrepreneurs have the willingness and ability to delegate, and they also view expenses differently. They consider the return on investment much more than the cost.

> You need to know how to view costs in your business or in your development. View it as a return on investment. If you pay someone $1, you should expect $3-5 back.
> *—JV Crum III*

Successful entrepreneurs also take ownership of their niche and pride themselves on being the best at whatever it is that they do.

> I encourage people to build up authority: speak at events, write books, learn and share what you know as a thought leader in your micro-niche. That's how you get well known faster.
> *—Richard Wilson*

Make Money, Live Wealthy

No matter what your career is, go pro! Have that mindset of being the CEO of You. Take absolute ownership and dominate your job or niche. Build that unstoppable mindset, leverage yourself by allowing others to do work you don't have to do, surround yourself with winners and advisors you trust . . . and always be hustling.

Entrepreneurship is a grind. It requires hard work and fighting fear. It necessitates putting yourself on the line and leaving your comfort zone on a regular basis. It calls for going out and doing things that others won't.

Michael Kawula shared a powerful story about hustling. When he was 20 years old, he went out one night. When he came home, his father was asleep—and never woke. Before he passed away that night, he left Mike a letter. In the note, Mike's dad quoted Abraham Lincoln:

> "Things may come to those who wait, but only the things left by those who hustle."

Mike has been hustling and succeeding ever since. If you really want something, you have to go get it. Going pro allows you to create the future that you want instead of waiting for it to magically occur. Hustle and fight through the fears and obstacles standing in your way.

> What differentiates successful entrepreneurs from everyone else is their willingness not only to *face* fear, but also to *embrace* fear. If you're not really scared of what you're doing, that means you're not pushing the envelope, you're not challenging yourself. It means you've moved into the right lane of the highway and hit cruise control, and there are cars zipping by you.
> —*John Dumas*

You *should* be scared! Embrace that fear. Push the limits of the possible. Don't be afraid of failure because there really is no such thing.

> I don't consider myself ever failing. I consider myself working hard at finding solutions. Failure has never been part of my mental makeup. It's always been a learning experience and digging deep to finding solutions.
> —*Larry Stevens*

Chapter 8: Entrepreneurial Success

It's only failure if you let it be failure. Use challenging experiences as your greatest lessons and opportunities for improvement.

It is all about how you perceive it. Expect challenges, fears, and failures—and embrace them. Act in spite of them. This draws the line between the entrepreneurs who fail and those who succeed.

> Put a process in place that allows you to make proper decisions. I keep a journal and write my thoughts as the day goes by. I will not make a decision on the same day. I put it in tomorrow's system, review it, and go through the process to make the appropriate decision. Journaling and creating a great plan are ways of eliminating the self-doubt on your business journey.
> —*Larry Stevens*

Consistency and making decisions move your business forward. Execution is key.

> The keys to success as an entrepreneur are: 1) Execution. 2) Pick a market that is big enough to offer a big pool of potential customers. You don't need a new idea; you just need to execute well in the right market.
> —*Neil Patel, serial entrepreneur*

Focus on building a solid business from Day One. If you have a good formula, you can succeed.

JV Crum said that the best advice he ever received was to focus on the bottom line. As soon as he started to think about how every decision impacts the bottom line, he turned his father's struggling business into a massive success.

> Every entrepreneur, every business, and every market will have a day in the sunshine. There will be good times, but you have to survive long enough to enjoy them.
> —*Trevor Blake*

Skills of a Successful Entrepreneur

The successful entrepreneurs had many skills in common, but a few skills of critical importance are listed below.

Sales

One skill can make or break a successful entrepreneur—the ability to sell. So many people have this fear, and it holds them back from even trying!

> No one actually fears selling. If you say you don't like sales, what you're really saying is that you fear *not selling*. Everyone loves to sell stuff and help people. 'What do I do when they don't buy?' That's what you can't stand. That's what you're afraid of. With that in mind, you have to make the appropriate adjustments.
> –*J. Massey*

So, what are some of the secrets to sales success?

- First, create something that is valuable.

  o "That was the great thing about my start because I learned early that if you can create something that's valuable, then it makes the selling part very easy." – *Kevin Johnson, entrepreneur and author of* The Entrepreneur Mind

- Focus on your customers and solve their problems in an authentic way.

  o "You can't build your wealth without learning how to sell in a meaningful way." –*Josh Brown*

- Focus on the process, not on the results.

  o "The number one key to success in selling is to be committed to your process every day without being emotionally attached to your results. This was the game changer for me. I became more consistent. Selling became easier and not stressful. If you're *emotionally attached* to results, you'll get discouraged. If

things go well, then you'll actually take your foot off the gas. Either way, your results suffer if you're emotionally attached."
—*Hal Elrod*

- And always listen . . .

  o "We spend and invest way too much time in talking, where the secret is really figuring out what to ask. Your customer or potential customer has all the answers." – *J. Massey*

J. Massey learned the hard way that listening was the most important skill. He shared the story of how he was talking to a prospect, and he was full of excitement . . .

> I talked and talked for I'm not sure how long. When I was done, he just simply asked me, 'Do you want to be successful? Do you want to sell stuff?'
>
> I said, 'Yes, of course. I'm talking to you, aren't you going to buy?'
>
> And then he said, 'You need to learn to say less to more people.'
> —*J. Massey*

Massey now suggests the 70-30 rule, which means that the customer talks 70% of the time. "When you follow that, you've got a plan," he says.

Sales done right doesn't look like sales at all.

> If we're doing it right, we're essentially doing four things: we're listening, we're teaching, we're communicating, we're helping.
>
> Can you hear the questions, concerns, issues, the problems of your prospects and customers better than anybody else in the world? Can you communicate in a way that they'll understand you? Do you see yourself as a teacher who's willing to answer anybody who has their hand raised? Do you see yourself as a problem solver? If you do, there's a very good chance you can crush it.
> —*Marcus Sheridan, entrepreneur and speaker, known as The Sales Lion*

Make Money, Live Wealthy

Marketing

> Seventy percent of a buying decision is made before the first contact—
> before they walk into your store or call you or fill out a form online.
> Basically, marketing is more important than sales.
> —*Marcus Sheridan*

Marketing and sales go hand-in-hand, and both are absolutely critical.

To do the best marketing, you have to think differently. Headsets.com CEO Mike Faith does this very well. Some of the different things his company does:

- "Last year a guy, Jason Sandler, was selling his last name off to the highest bidder. We were the highest bidder, and he became Jason Headsets.com for a year.

- We often send free gifts—usually headsets—to politicians, who then had to declare it on what gifts they've received.

- We put Tootsie Rolls in every package. We are the second biggest buyer of Tootsie Rolls in the world. It's a small thing, but people remember it uniquely. Do unique extra things for your customers to add value so that they'll remember you."

At the end of the day, it is all about people, people, people.

> I defy anybody to tell me anything in business that isn't related to people. What is marketing? It is predicting the behavior of other people. Sales is predicting the behavior of individuals.
> —*August Turak*

Find people, listen to them, help them, and the results will be everything that you desire.

Chapter 8: Entrepreneurial Success

Communication

> I think that we all need to become incredible communicators. We live
> in a time where people are thirsting for leaders who can distill their
> thoughts in such a way that everybody nods their heads and says, 'Yes!'
> If you can communicate about the thing you do in a way that everybody
> understands it, in a way that the light bulb comes on, you're going to be
> successful.
> —*Marcus Sheridan*

Being able to communicate well functions in much the same way as money
does: it makes everything else much easier. As a result, it is a skill that the
wealthy try to master.

Why does it matter so much?

> People are emotional creatures. Leadership relies on persuasion. You
> have to be able to persuade people. Persuading is being able to
> communicate effectively, and storytelling carries that emotional impact.
> —*August Turak*

You should leverage your strengths, but if any of these three areas are
weaknesses for you, it is probably best that you address them head-on and try
to become excellent at each one. If you do, there are no limits to the results
that you can achieve.

Scale & Sustain

The best way to scale something is to focus your attention on a small number
of things. If you spread your efforts too thin, you can be good, but not great,
at any of them. In the business world, the key is to find and leverage your
strengths. In doing so, you will see explosive growth as an entrepreneur.

Mike Michalowicz told about how he came up with a concept for massive
growth after being introduced to farmers of colossal pumpkins.

> By changing just a few things, the farmer causes the pumpkin to
> respond with explosive growth.

Similarly, an entrepreneur needs to focus on his strengths. Colossal entrepreneurs focus on their strongest customers. They try to clone their best customers. Likewise, they identify their best employees and try to clone them and cater to them.

Get rid of the weak ones. Weak customers and employees take a disproportionate amount of energy, time, and focus.

The colossal entrepreneur has the discipline to cut away the weak ones because they are stealing the energy from the colossal ones. The colossal entrepreneur has the discipline to say *No* to a lot of things so he can protect the one great thing: the colossal pumpkin.
—Mike Michalowicz

This discipline and focus will bring you the greatest success and freedom. Always remember the big picture and try to create something that will help you achieve exactly what you want. If your goal is complete freedom, build something that will help get you there. Focus on those strengths and delegate as much else as you can. Many people jump into entrepreneurship but end up creating more work for themselves than they had ever imagined.

Don't build a job. Build a business.
—Josh Brown

The things that can be scaled are not attached directly to your time. Dr. Dennis Cummins said the turning point in his business was after he'd received some training on how to systemize his business. Prior to this, his business was good, at best. Now it has grown, and it excels with very little interaction from him.

If you want to be successful, find a way to duplicate yourself. You need to find a way to back out and allow somebody else to take over. The more you can duplicate yourself, the more you can get done, the more lives you can change, the more products you can sell.
—Chris Locurto

Mike Michalowicz has done a lot of work with systemization and has written about it in several of his books.

Chapter 8: Entrepreneurial Success

Your business should be able to attract prospects, convert those prospects to clients, collect revenue from them, deliver your offering to them, and have them raving about you—all while you're sleeping. A business should be able to go full cycle without conscious input from the entrepreneur. When your business can do that, you have a business that you can scale to any size.

Systemization is focusing on every element of the business so you can ultimately remove yourself as the entrepreneur.

It's a time-consuming, meticulous process. Start off building the easiest system, the one that will take you the least amount of time. It may not offer you huge benefit, but it will build your confidence. When you see that it runs on automatic, you'll start building your system muscles and then be able to build the next ones.
—*Mike Michalowicz*

Begin with the end in mind and always be driving towards that vision. It may take some work, but anything is possible when you are in control of your own fate.

Summary

A. Entrepreneurship should be strongly considered by all.

Every single one of the experts interviewed is an entrepreneur. If you want to make the most impact or the highest earnings, then some form of entrepreneurship should be your choice.

I've not found one single mutual firm, one single real estate investment, any gold, silver or anything else that has given me higher returns than:

1) Me, investing in myself.

2) Starting a new business.

Go start a business. Go learn a skill set and become the best you can in that space. And look at the amount of money that people are willing to pay for the value you bring to the table. There's no other opportunity better than that to create wealth—not small wealth, but *real* wealth.
—*Patrick Bet-David*

Regardless of whether you become an entrepreneur or not, the mindset that you have from becoming the CEO of You will have an enormous and positive impact throughout your career.

B. The first thing you need to do as an entrepreneur is solve a problem.

The best way to start with entrepreneurship is by solving somebody else's problem. Ideas are everywhere—you just have to keep your eyes open and start to think like an entrepreneur. Think about:

- Problems you've had yourself.

- Inefficiencies you see in the workplace.

- Things that have not yet been created yet, but should be.

- How to connect the 'little guy' to the 'big guy.'

- Unique skills you have and how you can use them to help others.

Many people find the best ideas in things they are very familiar with. These ideas come from learning a segment inside and out and then finding a gap or an area for improvement.

> First emulate. Then innovate.
> – *Richard Wilson*

C. A big key to success is being niched in the right market.

Jump on a rising market and "ride the wave." From there, niche down, niche down, niche down.

> Find your niche, be clear about your proposition, and take action.
> –*John Murphy*

As Mike Faith says, "Pinpoint some portion of the customers within a market and cut off that section." Become the voice of authority to them and be very clear about who you are, what you offer, and what your business does—inside and out. Find a blend of your own skills and strengths mixed with a solution to a clearly defined need, and you have a recipe for success.

Chapter 8: Entrepreneurial Success

Niche down to a point where you have very few competitors. If you
can define a tight enough niche, then you can become known as a
household name in that tiny niche.
—Richard Wilson

Not only do you need to know what your business is, you need to know who
you are and align the market's needs with your skills, passions, and strengths.
As Matt Shoup said, "Entrepreneurs are superheroes." Find your superpower
and leverage it.

The difference between good and extraordinary is a very fine line. Focus on
the important stuff, leverage your strengths, and cut out the activities, people,
and customers that are holding you back. If you do so, you can become a
colossal entrepreneur.

D. You have to give before you receive.

Value has to come from you first, and that value gets returned back to
you.
—Ann Wilson

It is all about continuing to provide more and more value. Impact and
influence drive earnings, so focus on making the biggest impact and having
the most influence in people's lives.

Don't focus on the result—focus on the reason for the result. The wealthy are
selfless, giving, and mission-oriented first, and they know that these things are
the reason for their success.

The secret in life is to take this transformational journey because in the
long run, the more selfless you are, the more successful you are. It is in
your own self-interest to forget your self-interest.

The shortest distance between two points is actually the longest way
around because it is by getting away from yourself and going out and
getting selfless with other people that wealth comes back to you.

You don't know when and how this work is going to come back to you,
but it comes in unexpected and unbelievable ways.
—August Turak

E. It is all about hustling and failing forward.

The game of business is hard, and it requires focus and an attitude of success.

Challenges will arise, so you're going to have to do what Mike Kawula's father and Abraham Lincoln said to do: *hustle.*

Fear will rear its ugly head, failures will happen, but they are only temporary roadblocks, experiences, and lessons. Don't let them stop you. Learn how to embrace the unknown, and you can achieve such amazing things.

> There are three phases of uncertainty: fearing it, starting to overcome it, and then embracing it. There's a great quote from Tim Ferriss, "Most people will choose unhappiness over uncertainty," and it is this uncertainty that makes people unhappy. Once you get to a point where you *embrace* the uncertainty, you basically look at things and say, I don't know what's going to happen so I can make anything I want to happen. That is an entrepreneur's best friend.
> —*Sean Ogle*

F. Build a business, not a job.

It is all about creating the life and results that you want. You have to begin with the end in mind—which, I'm sure, doesn't have you doing more than you want to do. Build a business, not a job.

> You don't build wealth as a small business owner by going in and doing everything yourself and not putting in systems and processes. Don't just create a job. If you want to build wealth, build a business that is scalable or sellable.
> —*Josh Brown*

The systems are key. The goal is to scale and make a bigger impact—for others, as well as yourself. The way you do that is to learn how to take yourself out of the business and work *on* your business, not *in* your business.

Entrepreneurship is a challenging journey, but it's important to keep perspective and know what true success means to you.

Chapter 8: Entrepreneurial Success

The only measures of success I have are profit and fun.
—Trevor Blake

Entrepreneurship can provide the life of your dreams. It's not easy, but it can be simple . . . and it is most definitely worth it. Become the CEO of You and your career—and don't look back.

Action Items

1. Get the entrepreneurship guide at MakeMoneyLiveWealthy.com/chapter8. It includes my story of entrepreneurship and tips that I'd suggest you use early on!

2. Brainstorm and look for inefficiencies and problems that you can solve. Keep a journal of ideas and build on it consistently. Creativity is like a muscle—the more you work it, the stronger it becomes.

3. Start to become an entrepreneur (if you're not already), and start small. Dabble in something on the side and build it up. Doing this will not only supplement your income, but it will force you outside your comfort zone, build up more skills and connections, and allow you to do things you're passionate about—all at a low risk.

4. Begin with a vision! "You don't need money. What you need is vision. All businesses start with vision. Once you have a vision, then you can learn the skill sets necessary to attract all the other resources that are required." *—J. Massey*

5. Network with other entrepreneurs. The ideas, energy, and resources that will come to you by doing so are astonishing. It will help you see risk in a different light and motivate you to take massive action. Mike Faith said the number one trait that allowed him to be successful in business was networking. "Remember everyone you meet. Be nice to them because you'll need them one day—and even if you don't need them, you should still be nice to them." *—Mike Faith*

6. Regardless of what you do, always give value and always listen. The path to wealth is paved by helping others get what they want.

7. Once you're ready, *go pro!* Go all-in and create the wealth of your dreams.

8. "If you already have an existing business, identify your number one customer. The objective of every company is to clone its best client. Identify your best client, get in their minds, and understand them better than they do. That will be the gateway to finding more clients." *–Mike Michalowicz*

CHAPTER 9: INVEST & GROW

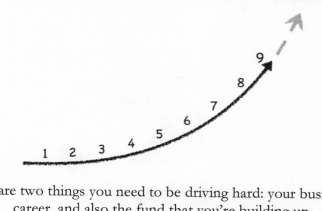

There are two things you need to be driving hard: your business or career, and also the fund that you're building up.
—*John Murphy*

The final piece to the wealth equation is to 'invest the difference wisely.' The wealthy focus not only on earning income, but on taking that money and growing it some more.

Non-Wealthy	Wealthy
Expenses > Income	Income > Expenses
or	AND
Expenses = Income	Invest the Difference Wisely

There are two reasons why investing is so powerful—the power of compound interest and the potential for unlimited earnings. Compound interest is the interest earned on the original investment plus all of the interest earned over time. It is basically interest that grows on interest—it grows exponentially.

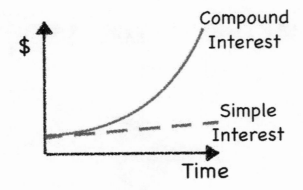

This can add up to amazing numbers over time. You may not feel the impact at first, but a small improvement in returns makes a dramatic impact in the long run. This is what separates the extremely wealthy from those who are just getting by.

Take the table below, for example. Assume you invest $10,000 per year (and no taxes for the sake of simplicity). You can see how compound interest adds up to some incredible numbers fairly quickly.

Compound Interest at Work

Annual Interest Rate:	3%	5%	10%	20%
5 Years:	$54,684	$58,019	$67,156	$89,299
10 Years:	$118,078	$132,068	$175,312	$311,504
20 Years:	$276,765	$347,193	$630,025	$2,240,256
30 Years:	$490,027	$697,608	$1,809,434	$14,182,578

Chapter 9: Invest & Grow

This is why you need to learn how to invest and start as early as possible. Investing $10,000 per year can fairly easily grow to $1,000,000, but the rate of return is very important. You may say that getting high returns is impossible and that twenty or thirty years is a long time, but it is absolutely possible to use investing—stock market, real estate, commodities—to see strong long-term returns. Twenty years from now, you will be extremely happy that you started building your fund as much as possible right now.

Waiting until later to start makes it drastically more difficult to build wealth. For example, assuming a 10% annual return on investment, if you start saving $10,000 per year at the age of 25, you will have $1,000,000 in your fund before turning 50. However, if you wait until you're 40 to start saving money, you will have to save nearly $60,000 per year to accomplish the same feat.

And remember, investments are earnings that you can build passively. Most people's investments are not their main income stream, but you can now see why it is an important third piece to the wealth equation.

> Young people think retirement is so far off, but after starting with $1600, I built a million-dollar portfolio before I turned 40. That gave me freedom to become an entrepreneur. It meant I didn't have to be stuck with golden handcuffs at a 9-5 job in the corporate world, which in my 40s didn't suit me anymore.
> —*Laurie Itkin*

Laurie accomplished this while working for someone else—in a completely unrelated field. Investing can be a great vehicle for anyone with any background.

> People assume that I am some financial wizard, but I'm not. I'm good, but not a wizard. You don't have to be a financial expert to achieve what I did. I had a different career as a policy advisor for a governor. I was not in a high-paying job until I became a lobbyist in my 30s.
> —*Laurie Itkin*

What we're looking for is freedom, and investing is an amazing opportunity that can give you the freedom to do what you wish with your time. Investing has enabled me to retire early, as well, so strongly consider really scaling the amount of money you put away and what you do with the money.

Risk-Reward

Given the amazing opportunity of investing, there has to be a catch, right?

There is. The catch is that investing can be quite challenging because:

- We're not built to be great investors.

  - Through millions of years of evolution, we are built to act on our emotions, and investing is a cycle of emotions. It is a never-ending battle of fear and greed, and a game against ourselves. You must have the discipline to not let these emotions alter your decisions.

- It takes time.

  - Many of us are not patient enough to do anything other than attempt to get rich quick or do something that gives us instant satisfaction (the paycheck route), but the way to true and massive wealth is through consistent action and time. This is how compound interest works its wonders.

- It requires effort up front.

  - If you go into investing blindly, you will do as Tom Basso says, and 'pay tuition to the college of trading'—also known as losing money. You have to learn some of the basics to avoid making the big mistakes that so many people make.

Poor Investor Mistakes

Most beginners make the same mistakes time after time (I know from experience). Here are some of the distinctions that separate those who make money from investing from those who don't.

Chapter 9: Invest & Grow

Beginner	Wealthy
Try to get rich quick!	There is no such thing as a get-rich-quick vehicle. Anything worth doing takes time. The way to wealth is to take care of the foundation, take care of the basics, and then build from there.
Listen to "hot" tips and chase returns.	"The first thing to be aware of is to invest for the long term. People might chase a specific trade, hoping that they instantly make a great return, but having the discipline and the focus to invest for the long term is a huge component." –*Ryan Michler*
Look to the news, TV, newsletters for investments to buy.	"Never listen to the media. Media is entertainment. Quality financial advice does not exist in sound bytes." –*Todd Tresidder*
Invest in countless things as soon as convinced by someone to do so.	"For new traders, focus on companies that you know and use in your daily life, companies that you understand." – *Patrick Schulte*
Don't plan for retirement and don't take advantage of tax benefits and 'free' money.	"Every time you make sure that Uncle Sam can't get your money, it really doesn't matter what investment you're in. You are making money just by virtue of not being taxed." –*Laurie Itkin*
Trade frequently.	The two biggest fees incurred from investing are taxes and commissions. As a result, the wealthy invest in a way that helps minimize these.

For most, investing will not be a career as much as it will be a second supplemental income stream used for retirement. In that case, you should have a long-term view and act accordingly.

Align Your Goals

Start with the end in mind—where do you want to go? Until you decide where you want to go, how in the world are you going to know how to get there? That will instruct you of what are the steps that you need to do to get there.
—*Jonathan Duong, financial planner, Founder and President of Wealth Engineers*

As with anything, the best way to succeed in investing is to figure out where you want to go and why you're going there. This will help you determine your style of investment, which investment vehicle to use, what level of risk you should expose yourself to, and how much time you need to spend managing your investments.

To help you with your goals for investing, answer these questions:

- Where does investing fit into your big picture plans? Are you investing for income, retirement, or excitement?

- When and how do you plan to retire?

To be successful with investing, you have to invest in ways that are aligned with your goals, personality, and risk tolerance.

If your financial goals are focused on being able to retire at a certain age, then you'll want to have a long-term perspective with your investments. If your goals are for income, then you'll want to learn more advanced trading strategies. The vast majority of people, however, should focus on simple long-term investments with their focus on creating income in their career or business.

Chapter 9: Invest & Grow

<u>Investment Avenues</u>

As you now know, taxes are the biggest expense that any of us will pay in our lifetime. In order to have the greatest long-term success, you need to be conscious of how you can benefit from different investment options. The ones that you choose should align with your financial position, career, and goals while minimizing the tax burden.

In the US, there are several retirement vehicles that offer tax advantages. The two key options are a 401(k) and an IRA (Individual Retirement Account). The amount of money that you can put toward these accounts is limited each year, but the value that you can gain is amazing. The earnings grow tax-free, and you can also avoid paying taxes on the front or back end depending on which type you choose.

1. 401(k)

The first place for most people to start investing is via a 401(k), a corporate-sponsored retirement plan.

In addition to saving on taxes, most companies offer a corporate match under a 401(k). This means that your company will add money into your account up to a certain amount. For example, if your company offers a 1% match and you put 1% of your salary into your 401(k), your company adds that same amount. So now you have 2% of your income going towards your retirement, but you only put in 1%. This is free money! The restrictions for the company match are that they are always capped, and you must invest some of your income or your company won't add the match.

> Start investing in a 401K as early as you can. With the company match, it's like a retirement account on steroids. They're going to pay you to invest in something you should already be investing in.
> *—J. Money, founder of BudgetsAreSexy.com*

- Who this is for? Anybody and everybody working for an employer that offers it. The tax benefits and 'free' money available are second to none.

Pros:

- You often get a corporate match up to a certain percentage (company adds to your account as long as you add money as well).

- You don't pay taxes on earnings.

- You can either use pre-tax money to fund the account, or you can choose not to pay taxes when you pull the money out in retirement if you use the Roth option.

- It is easy to set up and can be automatically deducted from your paycheck.

Cons:

- Only available if offered by employer.

- Limited options of what you can invest in (mutual funds).

- Money is held for retirement age; if you pull your money out before the age of 59 $1/2$, you'll pay taxes and a 10% penalty in most circumstances.

- No short selling, options, or individual stocks (other than company stock).

How to use it: If you have this option available to you, ask your HR representative how to get started. There will be a specified company that manages your 401(k), and you'll most likely set everything up online. You'll deposit money straight from your check to the retirement fund each pay period or as designated by you.

2. Roth IRA

IRAs are Individual Retirement Accounts that are independent of any employer-sponsored plan. These are available to most people in the US but have certain income restrictions.

Chapter 9: Invest & Grow

> Roth IRAs are ideal for young professionals because they can pay the taxes now, let the earnings grow tax-free, and never pay income tax during retirement.
> *—Steve Stewart*

Roth plans—whether Roth 401(k) or a Roth IRA—are great because they're another tax-advantaged account where, instead of saving on taxes today, you save on taxes when you pull the money out during retirement.

> 401k and Traditional IRAs are like paying for a tree; you'll save money on the taxes today, but you're going to pay the taxes on that million-dollar tree. When you forego the taxing today, as you do in the Roth IRA, you pay full price for the seeds, but you'll never pay for the million-dollar tree.

> For example, using compound interest over time, a $150,000 retirement account can grow into a million-dollar investment. Would you rather pay full price for the seeds today ($150k) or would you rather pay for the million-dollar tree?
> *—Steve Stewart*

Who this is for? Anybody, especially if you have a long time before retirement.

Pros:

- You don't pay taxes on investment gains.

- You don't pay taxes when you pull money out in retirement.

- Earnings grow tax free.

- You can withdraw contributions at any time (without the penalty).

Cons:

- Amount you're able to contribute is capped each year.

- If income is too high, you cannot contribute to a Roth.

How to use it: The easiest way is to open a Roth IRA through a brokerage account online or with the company that handles your 401(k). For more details, check out MakeMoneyLiveWealthy.com/chapter9.

3. Traditional IRA

A traditional IRA is similar to the 401(k) but lacks a corporate match. Its benefit is that you have many more options to choose from for your investments, and you use pre-tax money to fund it—the amount you put toward a Traditional IRA is not taxed until you pull the money out.

> A traditional IRA lets you choose from thousands of different mutual funds, not just the eight to twelve dozen that you have at your work plan (401(k)). You get more than one retirement account. Young professionals might have their own Roth IRA and then roll over an old 401k into a traditional IRA, but it's still better to have the control with that traditional IRA plan. It's likely that a young professional will change jobs quite a few times before retirement, so it would be nice to roll over all of those fractured 401(k)s and simplify your portfolio. Have your old company's benefits department help you with the paperwork.
> —*Steve Stewart*

Who this is for? Anyone looking to save for retirement who has maxed out his or her 401(k) match contributions, and if you believe your retirement tax rate will be lower than it is now.

Pros:

- Available to anyone (there are limitations based on earnings if they're very high).

- You don't pay taxes on contributions today.

- Gains grow tax free.

Chapter 9: Invest & Grow

Cons:

- You cannot contribute if your earnings are over a certain amount (see limitations at MakeMoneyLiveWealthy.com/chapter9).

- 10% penalty if you withdraw your funds before 59-1/2 years old. (There are exceptions where you can use these funds for college or a first-home purchase.)

- You cannot contribute after age 70 $^1/_2$, and you are required to take minimum withdrawals at that time.

How to use it: the same way as a Roth IRA.

4. Taxable Account

The first option that people often want to start with is a taxable brokerage account. However, this is typically the last place one should invest.

Taxable accounts should be used primarily under three circumstances:

- If you plan to pull the money out before retirement age.

- If you max out your other retirement vehicles (401(k) and IRAs).

- If you're trading for a living or want to sell stocks short.

Unlike the retirement vehicles, your earnings from a taxable account are taxed as normal income (unless you hold the asset for more than a year; then it is taxed as capital gains, which is almost always less than ordinary income levels).

The benefit of having a taxable account is the flexibility and the options available to you. You are much less restricted on what you trade, how often you trade, and how you do so (long, short, stock options).

Who is this for? Anyone who fits into one of the three circumstances above.

Pros:

- Complete flexibility of what you invest in (all stocks, funds, long and short, options).

- You can pull money out at any time without paying a penalty (as you would with the retirement vehicles).

Cons:

- Funded with taxed dollars.

- Pay taxes on gains.

How to use it: Open an account with an online brokerage firm such as TD Ameritrade, Scottrade, E-Trade, Vanguard or any of the many other options available to you.

Investment Vehicle Summary

	Fund With...	Earnings Grow	Withdraw During Retirement
401(k)	Pre-Tax	Tax-Free	Taxed
401(k) Roth	Taxed	Tax-Free	No Taxes
Roth IRA	Taxed	Tax-Free	No Taxes
Traditional IRA	Pre-Tax	Tax-Free	Taxed
Taxable Account	Taxed	Taxed	Taxed

Chapter 9: Invest & Grow

Each individual's situation is different depending on your financial position and goals, but below are a list of investing priorities that will be a good place to start for many.

1. 401(k) up to company match

   - The best way to start is always with free money! Save on taxes in addition to a potential match from your employer; that is as good a deal as you'll find anywhere.

2. Roth IRA

   - As Steve Stewart says, you can either pay taxes on the seeds or on the tree. I'll take the former.

3. Max Out Remaining Retirement Options (401(k), Traditional IRA)

   - You'll never regret planning for your future as early as possible, so put away as much as you can.

4. Taxable Account

   - Until you meet one of the three circumstances mentioned previously, it is best to steer clear of taxable accounts.

Choose a Strategy

There are countless strategies that you can implement to bring you a lot of success with your investments. The best strategy for one person may not be the best one for another person. Finding the right one for you relates back to your goals and personality.

What seems like a large, challenging task is actually quite simple when you take it one small step at a time.

My advice: let this be easy. Don't overcomplicate things. Put some solid strategies in place and stick with them.
—Ann Wilson

Here are some simple long-term strategies that the experts suggested.

Dollar Cost Averaging

> Dollar cost averaging is something wonderful and easy to set up. This is where you set a certain amount to invest every month regardless of what the stock market is doing.
> —*Brittney Castro*

What this does is take a lot of the emotion and guessing out of investing. For many of you, the goal is simplicity and a long-term return. Dollar cost averaging can be a great way to achieve both.

Who is this for? Someone who wants the simplest long-term strategy that takes essentially zero time and effort.

What you do: Set up a consistent dollar amount or percentage of income that goes directly to your investment fund (401(k), IRA, taxable account) and have the funds set up so that they purchase shares automatically (this is done in a 401(k)) or purchase the same amount of stocks and funds on a set basis (monthly, quarterly, or whatever you set). See an example of how this works at MakeMoneyLiveWealthy.com/chapter9.

Index Investing

Investing in index funds is another popular approach used by the YoPro Wealth guests. Index funds are an investment vehicle set to replicate the movement of a specific market index. They are most often a basket of a large number of stocks. Instead of buying one individual stock, you buy many at the same time. The key benefit of this is diversification for a lower price than if you bought each one individually.

> The best investment strategy is index investing. Rarely do managed funds do as well as index funds after three or four years. Over the longer run, you'll see very few that are beating index funds. The key is to keep costs down. With index funds, costs are 0.1%, while the average mutual fund investor pays 1.3%.
> —*Russell Wild, investment advisor, author of Index Investing for Dummies*

Chapter 9: Invest & Grow

Rob Berger says that the keys to successful investing are: 1) having a plan and 2) keeping costs low. To do that, he uses index funds to create the most long-term returns.

> My approach to investing is primarily a buy-and-hold long-term passive index fund portfolio. A well-diversified low-cost fund should be the core of your portfolio. I do long-term buy-and-hold Vanguard index funds to keep costs low.
> *—Rob Berger*

Fees and taxes are the two biggest costs that impact your investing (other than acting on emotions or without a plan), so if you can minimize those, you'll be well ahead of most.

Who this is for? Index investing is not available within a 401(k), but it is a great option in an IRA or taxable account. These are also a great option for anyone who doesn't want to merely buy and hold (although you could).

What you do: You can buy index funds in the form of ETFs (Exchange Traded Funds). These act like regular stocks on the American Stock Exchange, so you can purchase them like you would any individual stock. Examples of ETFs can include SPY (S&P 500 index fund tracks 500 widely held stocks), QQQ (follows Nasdaq-100 stocks), and hundreds of others including index funds by individual segment or industry. From there, you can choose from countless trading strategies that might work for you.

> Take it gradually. Start early, but start with a safer and more diverse portfolio. As you build confidence, you can move on to the more advanced side.
> *—Anton Ivanov*

Start off with a simple and consistent strategy and build from there. Focus on your priorities and move down the list as you add more to your portfolio. In addition, there are countless other advanced strategies that can be used for more active trading and investing.

<u>Manage Risk</u>

Anybody out there, if you're trading or investing, get this through your head: risk management is more important than anything else you could do. It is certainly more important than how you put on trades. It is the single most important thing there is.

—Jack Schwager, iconic investing author of the Market Wizards series

Traders will have different ways to manage risk, but if you're investing for the long term, here are five good ways to do so.

1) Diversify

If you diversify, go with the trend and manage your risk. Then it just has to work.

—Larry Hite (shared by Steve Burns)

Diversifying—not putting all of your eggs into one basket—is the most common and simple method of risk management. The more stocks or investments you have, the less one single stock impacts your returns. If you have a lot of stocks in your portfolio, then what happens with one stock won't likely affect your total fund too drastically . . . as long as you have proper position sizing.

2) Position Size

Position sizing goes hand-in-hand with diversifying. You never want too much of your portfolio put at risk by any one asset.

Look at how much capital you have. Say to yourself you're not going to risk more than 1% or 2% of the total capital on any single trading idea.

—Richard Weissman, author of Trade Like a Casino

This doesn't mean that you can only put 1% or 2% of your money into one stock. It means that you shouldn't *risk* that much. So let's say that you have ten assets in your portfolio using 10% of your total fund per stock or fund. If you want to risk no more than 1% of your portfolio, then you should not lose any more than 10% on a single stock or asset. The reason why is this—

Chapter 9: Invest & Grow

A 10% loss on 10% of your portfolio equates to 1%. This means you didn't lose 10%; you lost 1% of your total capital.
—*Richard Weissman*

By doing this, you cap the downside of your losses.

3) Asset allocation

Find your risk-return sweet spot; recognize how much 'heat' you can take.
—*Russell Wild*

If you're close to retirement and your focus is securing your assets, then you'll want to take less 'heat' and reduce your risk. If you have a long time to go before retirement, you may want to crank it up a bit and be more aggressive. Asset allocation is a great general barometer for how exposed you are to risk in the near term.

The key is to have an asset allocation plan split between stocks and bonds and stick with it, adjusted over time.
—*Rob Berger*

Asset allocation is often described as the percentage of your portfolio in stocks vs. bonds. For instance, someone who is a long way from retirement may have a small percentage of his portfolio (say, 10%) in bonds, and the rest in stocks. Bonds are perceived to be lower risk over the short term than stocks are, so someone closer to retirement may have well over half of his portfolio in these 'safer' investments.

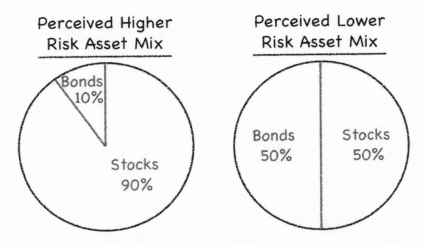

4) Rebalance

Once you have the proper asset allocation in place, you'll want to keep it that way. How you do this is by rebalancing your portfolio occasionally.

> Rebalance every year to get to the stock-and-bond mix that you see as suitable for your heat.
> —*Russell Wild*

The way this works is, for example, if you determine that the proper asset allocation for you is 50/50 (50% stocks, 50% bonds), you'll want to keep your portfolio at this mix. If your stock funds go up more dramatically than your bond funds, then the asset allocation will change and you'll be over-weighted towards stocks. To get back to the set amount of perceived risk that you want, you reduce your stock fund and increase your bond fund to get back to your 50/50 mix. That is rebalancing.

This is also done for the funds or stocks that you hold. You never want to be too over-weighted towards one thing, so rebalancing is a way to regularly keep your expected risk under control.

Chapter 9: Invest & Grow

5) Have a plan

The two most important things that you want to master are psychology and risk. The best way to do both of those things? *Have a plan.*

> The key to investing success, for me, has been to come up with a plan. If you take your future funding goals and compress them into a plan (how much you need to save this month), it opens up your mind and takes away all the uncertainty and fear.
> *—Jim Wang*

This was mentioned numerous times as the biggest mistake that most people make—*they don't have a plan!* If you don't have one, you make your decisions while things are happening—and we already know that we're emotional creatures who do not make good decisions in the heat of the moment.

> Here is another rule that works very effectively. Bruce Kovner, one of the great traders, said, 'Know where you're getting out before you get in.' That is the most important piece of advice anybody can give a trader or investor. The reason why it's important, beside the fact that it will limit what you can lose on any trade, is that before you get into a trade is the only time you have complete objectivity. Once you're in a trade, you're no longer objective. All sorts of emotions come into play; but before you get into the trade, you can think rationally. If you decide where to get out before you get in, that simplifies the process and provides very effective risk management.
> *—Jack Schwager*

Having a plan does two things to your investing:

1) It makes it boring (as the decisions are already made).

2) It helps make it much more profitable.

> Let your money and investing be boring. Get your thrills from creating and living a great life.
> *—Ann Wilson*

If you want thrills and excitement, you can get it with investing. However, if you want *profitable* investing, you'll probably have to go get your thrills elsewhere. The choice is yours.

Create a plan, and then let compound interest work its wonders.

> Once you've got this foundation and these systems in place, get out of the way and let it grow.
> —*Ann Wilson*

Just Start

> The keys to investing success are starting early, utilizing the power of compound interest, and being consistent.
> —*Robert Farrington*

The sooner you get over your fear of the unknown and get started, the better. Nobody ever wishes they hadn't started taking control of their financial future as soon as they did. In fact, most highlighted the fact that a regret they had was not starting even earlier!

> If I had been prudent with saving cash, more money could have been put to my portfolio and it could have multiplied when I was in my 20s.
> —*Tom Basso*

Save money now, so you don't have to worry later! Remember, every time you save, you are buying your future freedom.

Steve Stewart said to start with what you have, but try to sock away at least 10-20% of your income for your retirement. Laurie Itkin started out with a $1600 inheritance check. She turned that into over $1 million by the age of 40.

Patrick Schulte started out by selling his car to raise $5,000 to invest. He then retired at 29 so that he and his wife could sail around the world.

> Use time. Make it easy. Get your money to work for you. The key is to get in the market, as it is not about *timing* the market, but *time in* the market that matters.
> —*Ann Wilson*

Chapter 9: Invest & Grow

Compound interest is the most powerful force in the universe. You'll never be quite ready or know enough, so you just need to learn the basics and get started that you can let compound interest work its wonders.

<u>Summary</u>

Investing is an amazing vehicle to help you really grow your wealth; it should be an integral part of your financial plan.

The opportunity with investing is such that anybody can build a very large nest egg. The way you do this is through the most powerful force in the universe (compound interest) and your most valuable asset (time).

It does come with its challenges, however. We humans are built to be terrible investors, but successful investing is more than possible. It just requires the 5 P's:

1. Priorities

There are so many different ways that you can invest, but for the vast majority of people, investing should be used as a retirement vehicle and not a source of income. You should have a long-term view that aligns with your goals. The biggest expenses you'll incur with investing are commission fees and taxes. As a result, the wealthy trade in a way that minimizes these things. You should as well!

> It is very important to start early, take advantage of the way that US tax system is structured, take money and put it in your IRA or 401K, and start building your fund as soon as possible.
> —*Richard Weissman*

For the best and quickest returns on your investments, avoid taxes and take advantage of free money (company match in 401(k)). The order of investing priorities for most should be 401(k) up to the company match, Roth IRA, additional 401(k)/Traditional IRA, and then a taxable account.

Many want to get rich quickly, but the truth is that there is no such thing. Take a structured, intelligent approach to investing, and you'll be much better off.

2. Psychology

The two most important elements of investing or trading are 1) psychology and 2) risk management. We are emotional creatures, and the stock market is a never-ending balance of fear and greed.

You can manage your psychology and have much more profitable investing by 1) becoming self-aware and able to control those emotions or 2) taking the emotions out of it. One way to take the emotions out is to have a plan.

3. Plan

The single most important thing you can do is manage risk.

> Every successful trader will tell you that risk management is more important that the method. Most people focus on 99% on methods, 1% risk management, which is the source of a lot of problems.
> —*Jack Schwager*

Different ways to manage risk are to diversify, have proper position sizes so that you never risk too much, build the right asset allocation mix that aligns with what you want and can handle, and or rebalance on a regular basis. Basically, you want to have a plan for your investments.

A proper plan does a few things for your investments. It manages risk, makes it boring, and makes it more profitable.

> Investing done right should be as exciting as watching paint dry.
> —*Todd Tresidder*

4. Persistence

Having a plan isn't enough. You have to act with discipline and consistency. Investing is a long-term game that requires you to fight through the ups and downs—all the while keeping the big picture in mind.

Chapter 9: Invest & Grow

> You really need four things in order to be successful as an investor.
> You need to have time, desire, knowledge and discipline.
> —*Jonathan Duong*

When volatile or declining markets occur and emotions are running high, you must stay focused on the bigger vision and make conscious decisions that align with that. Jonathan also shared what Carl Richards calls, *The Behavior Gap*, where average investors end up significantly underperforming the total market because they end up doing the opposite of what they're supposed to do when emotions get involved.

Another key to being persistent is automation. You want to do as little work as possible, so set up your investments in such a way that you don't even realize the money is gone (i.e. direct deposit from your paycheck). You'll often be pleasantly surprised at what it adds up to over time without any interaction from you.

5. Patience

The most common mistake people make is to try to get rich quick. Good investing requires patience and time.

> I'd say that people who are successful in general certainly are those who use time to their advantage. Time is the single finite resource that, at the end of the day, we can't get back. So, starting early is absolutely a key component.
> —*Jonathan Duong*

Find a good system and stick to it. Remember, it is not 'timing,' it is 'time in' the market that matters.

Action Items

1. Investing from day one is how I was able to retire at the age of 27, so be sure to get the free investing resources and examples by going to MakeMoneyLiveWealthy.com/chapter9, which includes specific examples, training, recommended reading and the Invest Like a Pro ebook.

2. Create your investing goals and know how investing fits into your overall wealth plan. What is your time frame? What are you planning to achieve?

3. Set out your investing priorities and create a plan of attack. Where are you going to begin?

4. If possible, start investing in your 401(k) immediately and take advantage of the corporate match.

5. Identify a strategy and plan that works for you—*and just start!* Begin as simply as possible, and then if you feel inclined, move on to more advanced strategies from there.

CHAPTER 10: THE JOURNEY

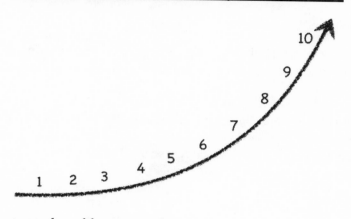

The journey toward wealth never ends.

It is a constant balance of many things while accepting the ebbs and flows that life brings you. As a result, this is the 10th and final element of obtaining true and massive wealth.

Time Matters

Time matters quite a lot, actually. It matters because:

1) Wealth Takes Time

> Wealth is not built in one day. It is a process that takes time and discipline.
> *—Erez Katz*

Nothing in this book is about a get-rich-quick scheme. True wealth takes time.

> Everybody wants the quick fix. It doesn't happen overnight. You have to be willing to put it out there. I call it 'the secret to being an overnight success,' which means there really isn't such a thing as an overnight success. The secret is you work really hard for 10 years, and then you become an overnight success.
> *—Jon Gordon*

Make Money, Live Wealthy

It takes years, and you most often don't see it in the moment. It is only those who persevere that will see their visions become realities.

2) The Real Education

It's in the movement; it's in the action that you learn what you need to learn. You can't learn it by planning. You're learning as you're going: *ready, fire, aim!*

> There are people who spend years trying to get it right. They try to make sure they have everything just exactly where it should be before they pull the trigger. Without jumping into the unknown and getting into action, it is hard to discover who you are as a human being.
> *—David Wood*

You're never going to be ready. You just have to have faith that it is going to work out, get over that first hump, and start. That is when the real education begins.

> Just go out and do it. Know that you're not going to be 100% sure, but you're going to learn along the way. The sooner you start, the more time you have to succeed.
> *—Matt Shoup*

3) You're Going to Fail

> Every one of our journeys is littered with failure. The sooner you can get those failures out of the way, the better.
> *—John Dumas*

This may be scary to hear, but you're going to fail at some things. It doesn't matter how well you prepare, there are going to be some stumbling blocks along the way. Just know that failure isn't as bad as many make it out to be; numerous guests said that the more they failed, the more they succeeded. Change your beliefs and fears about failure, and get into motion.

4) Time is Precious

We often don't realize this in the moment, but there is no commodity more precious than time. It is a limited resource.

Chapter 10: The Journey

Time is much more important than money because you only have so much of it. The tricky part is that, as a society, we focus a lot on money as the embodiment of wealth. When you're young, you think about money because you have very little of it, but you have a lot of time. It's a slow conversion as you get older. Your time shrinks and your wealth hopefully grows, and then time becomes the focus.

Once you've reached a certain level of wealth that correlates with your age, you don't really care about the money. You are about the time you have left and the relationships you have. Money stops mattering.
—Jim Wang

Your time is precious. Take advantage of it now, so you don't have to regret it later.

It is never too early or too late to start chasing your dreams. There is only one thing you can control, and that is the decisions you make.

It's never too late to have a new beginning. It's thrilling to see people who maybe are approaching what they thought was retirement, and they start to really come alive with the dreams that have been buried for so many years. It doesn't matter if somebody's 18 or 88, tomorrow's going to be a new day.
—Dan Miller

Don't wait and see what happens. Go and create the life you want to have tomorrow today.

5) Compound Effect

Every decision matters. Every decision adds up to create what we call *the present*. To change your future, you have to change your decisions now.

Nothing is ever neutral; everything counts. Everything matters. Make sure you're doing things every day that move you forward. Make sure your mindset is about going out and being the best that you can be every day.
—John Murphy

Make Money, Live Wealthy

It may not feel like it at the time, but your decisions all add up. One small decision after the next adds up and creates a massive impact. One good decision alone won't make you a millionaire, but one good decision after another after another will add up to some amazing things.

> How you make your decisions over the long run start adding up in one direction or another. They benefit you and your long-term plan, or they get in the way.
> —*Tom Basso*

Compound interest is the most powerful force in the universe. It doesn't matter if it is with investments or with your own personal skills, the key to success is one small step after the next after the next.

> The way compound interest works is: the longer you do something, the greater the return.
> —*Erlend Bakke*

Start, fail, learn, improve, and always keep moving forward one decision at a time.

Fear No Fear

To stay the course and become completely wealthy, you need to accept the challenges that go along with it. The two inevitable things that you'll experience during your journey are fear and failure.

> Fear never goes away. Don't let it control you.
> — *Michael Kawula*

Everyone experiences fear. Whether you're at the beginning of your journey or already ultra-wealthy, fear will always threaten to hold you back. No matter what level of success someone has attained, there are always doubts about the next level.

> Life can be dangerous; just let it be. When we shake off what we perceive as our boundaries, that is where the bliss really is.
> —*Ann Wilson*

Chapter 10: The Journey

Act in spite of fear and use it as your motivation. Mike Michalowicz said he was fear-driven for a long time. The way that he squashed those fears was by hustling, and then hustling some more.

> Fear hates community. Fear hates action.
> —*Jared Easley, entrepreneur and coach, host of Starve The Doubts podcast*

Fearlessness isn't the absence of fear. It is merely embracing fear and not letting it stop you from your success. Once you can act regardless of fear, then you have absolute power. Be fearless.

Fail Forward

Failure happens to everyone, especially to the successful!

> The road to success is paved with failure. I fail on a daily basis.
> Unfortunately, we have a negative neuro-association to the idea.
> —*J. Massey*

One common trait among the wealthy is how they view failure. It's only a failure if you accept it as such. It's not a true failure if you get something from it.

Jack Schwager, who has interviewed many investing icons since the 1980s, has said that their stories are littered with failure. They started, failed early, and then moved on. They don't view failure as a bad thing.

> Another important thing, it goes to the heart of the way we view failure as a culture, the way we view failure in our educational system—this idea that failure is something horrible and bad. Of course nobody wants to fail, but the reality is that much progress comes from failure. The people who really succeed go out of the box and do stuff that will make them more likely to fail, but they ultimately succeed because they are willing to do that. They're willing to take that unconventional path or try something different. Failure is part of an evolutionary process, a necessary step to ultimate success. Failure itself, how you fail, makes you wiser, better, and stronger.
> —*Jack Schwager*

Success ultimately comes from failure.

> Failure is always a part of our journey. The more I fail, the more
> success I seem to have.
> —*Brittney Castro*

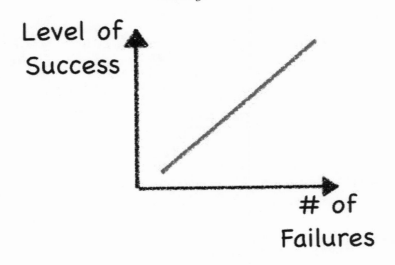

You just have to be sure that the failure is not catastrophic. The key is to manage your risk so that the failures remain small, and you can come back quickly.

> It's important to know that it's not a matter of whether you're going
> to fail, but how you recover. Every day, put on your problem-solving
> hat because that's what you are: you're a problem solver.

> Wealth is not about doing everything perfectly; it's about being able
> to persevere and make those painful moments be as short-lived as
> possible so you can keep moving on.
> —*Justin Williams*

It doesn't matter what the mistake is or how big it is. The wealthy experts all failed and overcame some massive challenges.

- Justin Williams' business was quickly $120,000 in debt.

- Matt McWilliams faced 42 years in prison.

Chapter 10: The Journey

- Ruben Rojas became a millionaire by 23 and lost it all by 27.

- Hal Elrod was considered clinically dead for six minutes.

It doesn't matter what the challenge is, you can get back up and move on to achieve massive wealth.

Hal Elrod was hit head-on by a drunk driver at the age of 20. He was pronounced dead for six minutes, but was eventually resuscitated. After being in a coma for six days, he was told that he might never walk again. To prove them wrong, he not only walked again, but he went on to complete an ultra-marathon. He is on his path toward wealth, and he isn't getting off of it.

If he can do it, is there any question that you can overcome your own challenges and obstacles in life? I know you can.

> A lot of things that may seem like they're there to tear you down are actually there to help build you up in different ways.
> *—Pat Flynn*

Winners not only turn failure into experience; they turn it into motivation. Matt Shoup went from being fired to creating a multi-million dollar business. Mike Michalowicz regretted quitting his job—after drinks—but continued on to be a massive success.

Ryan Holiday shared the stoic exercise of framing obstacles as opportunities from his book, *The Obstacle Is the Way*.

> The stoics believed that we don't control the world around us; we only control our response to the world around us. Specifically, when unpleasant things happen, we have the ability to respond positively.

> The stoics said, 'The impediment to action advances action. What stands in the way becomes the way.' When something bad happens, you can respond in a way that makes it positive. Every situation you face is a chance to practice excellence in a new form.
> *—Ryan Holiday*

Use every event, be it good or bad, as an opportunity to learn and improve. We may not be able to control the world around us, but we can control how we respond to it.

<u>The Marathon</u>

It's a marathon. Find ways to build your wealth one step at a time.
Don't try to 'break the bank' in one shot.
—Erez Katz

Success takes time. It doesn't take days or even weeks—it takes years.

It took me five or six years before I started getting momentum. Before that point, I was trying to be everything to everybody. I realized that by being diluted like that, I wasn't special for anyone. When I started focusing on hedge funds, I started getting calls from everyone in that industry, and my business started growing explosively.
—Mike Michalowicz

Numerous entrepreneurs shared a five-year time frame before things really started taking off. That is the turning point for many businesses.

I know it's scary, but that doesn't mean you shouldn't try—it just means that you should expect a bit of a grind. Our level of fulfillment is often a reflection of our reality compared to our expectations, so expect a battle! Be prepared for the challenges.

Do the best you can wherever you are because somebody's going to see you shining, and somebody's going to take you away from that junky place that you're in. Stay focused every single day on doing the greatest job that you possibly can. If you're diligent, you will prosper.
—Chris Locurto

If you persevere, you can do anything. J. Money is living proof of that.

Once you set your mind to it, stick to it, and pour your heart into it, anything really does become possible.
—J. Money

Chapter 10: The Journey

That is what it's all about. Searching, learning, challenging, and pushing yourself to places you'd never have thought possible. And any person who has achieved true wealth will tell you that it is all worth it.

> Success is in the journey, but the reward is the view from the top.
> —*Larry Stevens*

The only way to get that view is to be on a path that is true to you.

> Wealth is holistic. The only way that you can experience your journey is to be present. You need to have the journey that's right for you. If you miss your real journey, you miss your real life.
> —*JV Crum III*

The journey to become wealthy not only takes time, but it never ends. It isn't a destination; it is a state of mind and a belief that comes from being on the path that is true to you.

> As long as you're on that journey, you're on your way to true wealth. Once you've tasted what it's like to be on your journey, whatever that is, you can't get off of it.
> —*Josh Brown*

SUMMARY

10 Simple Steps

There are ten steps to true wealth. That's it. Succeed at accomplishing each step, and wealth is yours.

1. Take Control

Before you get anywhere, you have to make the decision and commit to it. Most people say they want something, but they are never able to fully decide and commit to the goal. Not making that decision is a decision in and of itself.

> Wealth is a choice.
> —David Wood

What's happened in the past has passed. You can move forward and change the world, but first you must:

1) Take responsibility for your past, present, and future. Where you are today is a product of the decisions you have and have not made. Where you're going to be in the future will be a byproduct of the decisions you make from now until then.

2) Take control of your life—whether it be your finances, health, relationships, or any other important area of your life. You are in control.

You can delegate *authority*, but you cannot delegate *responsibility*. Nobody can get you where you want to go quite like you. Don't wait. Now is the time. Don't say, 'When I have money I will take it seriously.' It has to be the other way around. Take control now, so that money can come into your life and stay there.

2. Develop the Wealthy Mindset

> What is going on in my head will determine the actions that I take, and
> the actions that I take are going to determine the results that I get.
> —*John Murphy*

The mindset is everything. If you want to get rich, you have to think like the rich do.

This is the biggest challenge that most people have. Growing up in common society, we are trained to believe certain things. These beliefs hold us back from our ultimate success. We become our own greatest enemy.

The good news is that we can reprogram our minds for success. Our subconscious doesn't know time and can't recognize what is real or fake, so by implementing some healthy habits (affirmations, visualization), we can reverse our beliefs and create an unstoppable mindset.

There is nothing more important that you can do on your way to wealth.

3. Create the Right Environment

> Your wealth is going to grow when you grow yourself, and you are
> never too old to grow. Take 10% of your income and invest it in
> yourself: training programs, experiences or adventures, or anything
> else that's going to grow you.
> —*David Wood*

You become the person the environment around you makes you out to be. If you want to change your life, change your surroundings.

Your environment consists of the information you feed your head on a daily basis, as well as your network and the team around you. The wealthy know better than to try and do everything on their own— they have coaches for the important areas of their life.

The way to get through the tough times is to have a network to support and help you along the way. With a strong team of people around you, you will have the confidence to take on and handle risks, leveraging the knowledge and resources of these people instead of trying to be a superhero yourself, which saves a lot of time and effort.

It is well worth it to build an environment that is ripe for success. Several guests mentioned that this is the number one mistake that holds people back, so be sure to address it head on.

4. Build Your Financial Foundation

> The biggest mistake people make is that they don't take care of their foundation. They don't take care of the base.
> —*Ruben Rojas, financial coach, entrepreneur and athlete*

If you don't know what to do with your current finances, you aren't going to be able to handle more. It is very important to develop a strong foundation so that you can build and maintain massive wealth in your life.

A strong financial foundation consists of the right money situation (no debt, emergency fund, protections) and habits (savings, investing) that enable you to reach your goals. A strong foundation will not only give you the peace of mind that you seek, but also the preparation to be able to handle any setback that comes your way.

By creating a plan for your money and taking a structured approach, you take a shortcut to your goals. Wealth is not something that happens overnight, so a big-picture vision and methodical plan always works best.

5. Gain Clarity

> Clarity is power.
> -*David Wood*

If you know with absolute clarity where you're going—and why—it is a much, much easier process. You start to notice resources and opportunities, and you get less distracted by everything else that is going on.

Clarity comes from doing the introspective work and looking at your actions and your past to find trends, but also from taking action. You don't know what is going to work until you actually start down a path that's right for you.

Summary

You have to become clear on what kind of balance and lifestyle you want, how much money you want, and what the purpose for that money is. Then you can create goals and milestones to help get you to that destination. It starts with the end, and then you work your way backwards, creating the necessary steps from there.

Also, you must also be clear on your *why*. Everybody has a purpose—the key is to figure out what that is and use it as your driving force.

6. Find Your Dream Career

> The perfect combination is when you do what you love to do and it generates income for you.
> —*Rob Berger*

Success internally (happiness) comes from doing what you love and living out your passion, but success externally (money) comes from using your skills and solving other people's problems!

You're going to spend a lot of time working, so you might as well do something you love. A secret of the wealthy is: the more that you enjoy something, the better you become at it, which ultimately results in more money.

But passion isn't enough. To have something that is sustainable and makes you a lot of money, you have to do something at which you're skilled. Passion without a useful application doesn't get you very far.

The key is to find out how you can mix your passions and skills with a vehicle that fits who you are and the goals you have. The good news is that the options are endless. The key is to keep searching and trying until you find that perfect mix. Know that your career can change at any time, and use each experience as a stepping stone to get where you want to eventually be.

7. Make Money, Create Wealth

Money is only a tool, but it is a very important piece of the equation. It doesn't create wealth in and of itself, but it does help make everything that we really want much more possible.

Once you get the foundation in place, it's time to get into motion and go make some money. The best way to do that is by excelling at the wealth equation:

Make more money than you spend, and invest the difference wisely.

The wealthy focus on simplifying the process, having multiple streams of income, and chasing residual and passive income so that they can get paid as many times as possible with the least amount of effort. They focus on being selfless and making an impact on other's lives, but they start all of this off by thinking and believing big.

8. Succeed in Business & Entrepreneurship

Entrepreneurship is living a few years of your life like most people won't, so that you can spend the rest of your life like most people can't.
—*Anonymous (shared by Michael Kawula)*

Every single expert is—or was—an entrepreneur. To create massive wealth, you have to become the CEO of You, whether you work for someone else or not.

Entrepreneurship is challenging and can be a risky endeavor, but anybody can excel as his or her own boss. The secret is to be aware of who you are and the value you can best provide to the world—and leverage that as much as possible. The best entrepreneurs solve a specific problem and strive to be the very best in their specific niche.

The wealthy take massive action, and they fail forward fast. They still fail often, but the more they do so, the more they succeed. They view risk differently and understand the cost of doing nothing. As they grow, they work to take themselves out of the business as much as possible so that they can scale and have as much freedom as possible.

9. Invest & Grow

The best advice I received was to let this be easy. Don't overcomplicate things. Put some solid strategies in place and stick with them.
—*Ann Wilson*

Summary

The final piece to the wealth equation is to 'invest the difference wisely.' Compound interest is known as the greatest force in the universe, and the wealthy know how to take advantage of it. It can be used for you or against you—you decide.

The easiest way for most people to invest is through the stock market. Investing has a high reward, but it comes with risk because we are not built to be great investors. The stock market is a measure of human psychology and involves so many emotions. To excel, you must take those emotions out of the game and approach investing objectively.

The best way to get started is to keep things simple and consistent and let time work its wonders. From there, if you have the interest, you can move on to more advanced strategies. The key, however, is to align your strategy and plan with your goals, keep costs low, and get started as soon as possible. If you can invest with a long-term view and manage risk and consistently add to it, you can set yourself up very well financially by investing on the side. As with anything, it just takes starting.

10. The Journey

> The biggest lesson is live your life now; live it in a way that really supports you.
> —*Ann Wilson*

Wealth is not a destination or a certain amount of money that you have to have, but more of a constant balance and journey of growth.

Along the way there will be many fears, doubts, and failures. But wealth is a long-term game that takes perseverance and necessitates living in a way that consistently propels you forward. You must accept the ebb and flow of life and the fact that you don't have to know the answers or be perfect, and you must always be willing and able to adjust your course as necessary.

Time is one of the most important ingredients of getting to where you want to go. It's a marathon, not a sprint, and successes don't happen overnight—they take years. The way to achieve your dreams is to always keep your vision in mind, as well as a perspective on what is truly important to you. The joy does not come from the external rewards you gain, but from who you become and who you help others become along the way.

Every step matters. It all adds up—the good and the bad—to the sum of your life. The beautiful thing is that you control those decisions. Complete the 10 steps, and wealth is yours.

How to Get Started

I've offended more than one person by getting in his face and letting him know: nothing changes until you start.
—J. Massey

So, you've learned a lot about what wealth is and how to obtain it. Now is the time to get into motion.

A lot of the experts interviewed had a surprisingly common regret—they wished they had started sooner. Whether it be their business, their new career, or their finances, they wished they had taken control and initiated action much sooner.

Everything is just a dream until you make it real. Reading this book does you no good unless you do something about it.

Just start. Successful entrepreneurs are successful because they were, at one point of their lives, willing to start. They were willing to give up things for the greater good, building a life they could be passionate about, a life they could be proud of, a life that would give them the freedom that they wanted.

Carve out some time in your day, and just start.
—John Dumas

It is important to start sooner rather than later because the greatest asset we have is time. Don't delay; get headed toward wealth right now.

The bottom line is that you start now. Life is now, and it is about urgency. Just go. Take committed action, and make it happen.
- Ruben Rojas

Summary

Here are seven actions to get started with on your journey to wealth.

1. Simplify

> Simplicity is the ultimate sophistication.
> —*Neil Patel*

The only way to achieve huge goals in your life is to break the tasks down into manageable chunks. There is a lot of information in this book, and it can be overwhelming. What you have to do is simplify.

> If you make $100,000, that puts you in the top 10% of all wage earners—but making $100,000 is nothing more than a thousand people paying you $100, or 100 people paying you $1,000. If you wanted to make more money than nine out of 10 of your friends, all you need is to come up with a product or service for which 100 people will pay you $1000 a year, $80 a month, or $20 a week. That's doable and is not that far away.
> —*Rob Wilson*

Take it one step at a time. Identify where you are in the process and start from there.

> The most important thing is getting started. Many people say, 'I want to build a resort or I want to do apartment buildings.' That's great, but that's not likely where you're going to start.
> —*J. Massey*

Just start from where you are and then do as John Lee Dumas says and FOCUS: *follow one course until success.*

2. Ask for Help!

Don't be afraid to ask for help. Success breeds success, so find people who are getting the results you want and ask them questions. Hire them as coaches, join their groups, and sign up for their newsletters. Do whatever you can to learn from them.

> Find somebody that will work with you, challenge you, and give you
> guidance. Find somebody who's been down the road before, somebody
> who can really mentor you and help you develop because it's not just
> about growing your income; it's about growing yourself.
> *—John Murphy*

One thing that you must take away from this book is that in order to be your best, you need a coach. Every single expert has one (or more) for a reason.

It's hard to achieve big things on your own—so don't. By leveraging the experience, knowledge, and networks of others, you press the fast forward button on your way to wealth.

3. Be Grateful

Gratitude is one of the many secrets of the wealthy. A lot of super-successful people start their day off with gratitude because it gets the positive energy in motion.

> Have gratitude for where you are, no matter where that is. Be really
> clear about where you want to go, and just take one step toward that
> goal each and every day.
> *—Dr. Dennis Cummins*

Matt McWilliams and August Turak also gave us their top tip for success: write thank-you letters. It's simple, yet more impactful than you could imagine.

> It takes five minutes to write a thank-you note. But research suggests
> that writing that note will give you a 31% increase in productivity over
> the next three hours. You also get the added benefit of affecting their
> lives, which in many cases will benefit you in return.
> *—Matt McWilliams*

Summary

4. Get Your Reason Why

> If you want something, you need to have a *why* big enough to push you through. You have to sell yourself on why it's important because if you don't have the strong reason why, at the first sign of challenge, you will give up.
> —*Peter Voogd*

When in doubt, go back to your vision. Go back to the reason why you're doing what you're doing. Go back to the result you'll achieve if you keep on going.

A big enough *why* can overcome any *how*. Most people don't take action because they don't have a strong reason why. There isn't any urgency to fight through. You need to be clear on what your real goals are. The clearer you are, the smoother the ride will be along the way.

> Have that mission statement—a clear guiding purpose that moves you so much that you're willing to sacrifice and do the hard things so that you can get to where you want to go.
> —*JD Roth*

You have a responsibility. You were put on this earth for a reason. Your responsibility is to find out what that reason is and see it through.

5. Be Okay with Failure

> I need you to get six F's really fast. I need you to Fail Fast, Fail Forward, and Fail Frequently. That is the best teacher, *period*, because through experience you will learn about yourself, about character, and about people. The wonderful lessons you learn can become some of the greatest springboards for your best business ideas.
> —*J. Massey*

Remember, wealth is a state of mind. Part of that belief is accepting that things aren't going to be perfect and being flexible enough to adapt to the ups and downs while always moving forward.

Make Money, Live Wealthy

The successful are the creative minds, the ones who are willing to be imperfect. They're in this constant Thomas Edison mode of experimentation, and they're embracing the failures probably more than the actual successes.
—Marcus Sheridan

You'll never take a single risk if you think one failure will ruin what you've worked hard for. Figure out what the worst-case scenario is and accept that. Then improve from there. The time will never be right, but develop a mindset where you expect and welcome any challenges that come up, and you'll be much better prepared to handle them.

6. Continue to Invest in Yourself

Success leaves clues, and it's everywhere. Just model success and continue to model success.
—David Wood

Even with the magnificent returns you can get in the stock market and real estate, everything pales in comparison to the returns that you get by investing in yourself.

If you want to build more wealth and grow yourself as a person, first you need to invest in yourself. You need to spend money, but it's not spending money when it's truly coming back to you. This is important to understand, or you'll always be struggling and living paycheck to paycheck.
—John Lee Dumas

Make personal development a habit. You'll be more than happy that you did.

7. Create the Environment for Success

Your network is your #1 key to success.
—David Wood

If you change your environment, you change your life.

Summary

By putting good information in your head on a regular basis and surrounding yourself with the right people, you reprogram your mind. It isn't a quick process, but everything you listen to matters!

Remove the negative from your life and replace it with positive. Replace it with information, people, resources and habits that will take you to the level of wealth that you want to reach. And by all means, stop taking advice from people who are not enjoying the level of success that you envy.

Create an environment that will help shape the person you want to become. Doing so is priceless.

> You have a choice. You can do anything you want. All you have to do is find the right vehicle, and then surround yourself with the right community. From there, wealth is yours.
> —*David Wood*

The 10 steps to wealth are easy, yet you need to take action now. Listen to the wealthy. Learn from those who are where you want to be and let them guide you. Don't try to achieve everything all at once, but do develop an environment that will help you prosper and move forward one step at a time.

True Wealth Summary

Always remember the goal. Define what true wealth is to you and go after it with all your might.

True Wealth is having an abundance of what you really want. It is being fulfilled in all the important areas of your life and having the proper balance for you.

It is complete freedom—the freedom to choose, the freedom to do what you wish, when you wish, with whom you wish. It is about having the flexibility and openness to change and adjust. It is about being free from worry and stress.

It is about having enough money, not for the sake of being rich but for the sake of living a rich life—one full of experiences and memories. It is about having enough money to provide you with security and peace of mind, as well as the freedom to pursue your dreams.

Wealth is a mindset, a belief, and a state of being. It is about having the knowledge of what true wealth is and how to obtain it, but also having the confidence and belief that you *can* obtain it. It is about getting out of your own way, thinking wealthy, and seeing the greatness in your everyday life.

True wealth is happiness. It is having the relationships and experiences that are important to you and the health to be able to enjoy it all. It is about family, love, connection, and community.

It is about living a passionate life that is true to who you are. It is about having a purpose and being on your true north. It is about making a contribution to society, impacting others' lives, and leaving a legacy that you're proud of.

Wealth is about continuing to learn, grow, and push yourself to new limits. It is about perseverance, overcoming obstacles, and moving forward through thick and thin. It is about doing the things that nourish your mind, body, and soul.

It is about accepting the journey, seeing the big picture, and enjoying the ride. It is about being present in the moment and grateful for the blessings of your life. It is about having a vision and seeing that through. It is about love, laughter, and living a life that is wealthy to you—now and forever.

That is what true wealth is.

This never-ending balance is what the wealthy master, and you can do the same. Remember, the experts interviewed are just normal people that have done extraordinary things by implementing the 10 simple steps laid out in this book.

<u>Enjoy the Ride</u>

Most important of all, *enjoy the ride.*

> The greatest lesson I've learned is to live life right now!
> —*Ann Wilson*

True wealth and happiness occurs in the present moment. You work hard, and you do so for a reason—to live the life you dream of living.

As long as you keep the big picture *and* the present moment in mind, you'll do great things and be living a wealthy life.

> Wealth is not about having a ton of money. It is about living richly, having a life rich in experiences, friendships, and relationships. It doesn't mean you don't have stuff. You have plenty of stuff. It just doesn't have *you.*
> —*Chris Locurto*

Keep everything in perspective. Work hard but remember why you're working.

> The idea of freedom and security isn't about sacrificing everything today because tomorrow never comes.
> —*Mindy Crary*

Get on the journey that is right for you, and you will never want to get off. If you know what it takes to become wealthy and believe that you can do so, you *are* wealthy.

> As long as you're on that journey that is right for you, you are on your way to true wealth. Once you know enough and once you've tasted what it's like to be on that journey, you can't go back.
> —*Josh Brown*

On his own show, David Wood asks each guest what a kickass life means to them. I turned the tables and asked David what a kickass life is to him.

> A kickass life is complete choice. It is the ability to wake up every single day and choose to do whatever you want, whenever you want. It

Make Money, Live Wealthy

is the freedom to look at the world as your playground, to look at
people as your greatest assets, to live an extraordinary life, to squeeze
all of the juice out and know you left it all on the field. It is to know
that I've laughed as hard as I can, I've cried, I've climbed the highest
mountains, I sang when I shouldn't, I break all of the freaking rules,
and I have a blast. And living a kickass life is being supremely kind to
every person, whether you get anything or not.
—David Wood

A kickass life is about more than money—it is about wealth. Actually, it is
about true wealth.

We all have this pen in our hand and this blank sheet of paper.
Whatever we want to write for ourselves is absolutely possible.
—David Wood

You now know what true wealth is and how to obtain it. The pen is in your
hand. Now it is time to go write your story.

Take Control. Make Money. Live Wealthy.

APPENDIX

I'm Proof

I'm living proof that these 10 steps can make you truly wealthy.

I started my journey at the bottom, just like everyone else I interviewed. In fact, I started out six years ago after college with $80,000 of debt. I had a lot of ambition, but I really knew nothing about the details or importance of any of these steps.

However, I learned from wealthy people I admired, and I implemented the things they told me in my life. I have failed often (and forever will) and was afraid for the majority of the journey, but I continued to move forward down my path toward wealth—one step at a time.

The result, as I said at the start of this book, is that I was able to 'retire' at the age of 27.

No, I don't have $10 million in the bank just yet, but more important than that, what I do have is freedom, peace of mind, passion, energy, health, an amazing network, and an unstoppable mindset—and these things are absolutely priceless.

I don't say any of this to brag (my biggest fear in life is to come off as a braggart); I say this to show you 1) that you can change, and 2) to show you how quickly things can change when you take the proper steps.

We always put off preparing for tomorrow, but the time has to be now. You won't feel change in the moment, but you will most definitely notice it after a short period of continuous action. I know from experience that the compound effect adds up quickly—financially and in every other area of life. It starts with a decision, and everything domino effects from there.

Let me leave you with four thoughts—

Make Money, Live Wealthy

Reading

Keep reading, keep learning. This was the first major step that started to change my mindset, and it happened one chapter at a time. I have many more books that I want to write in order to help you achieve your dreams—financially and beyond. My only goal is that these books will have the same impact on you as some books have had on me. There are a number of books that have changed my life. See the list and join our book club for free at MakeMoneyLiveWealthy.com/bookclub.

Networking

Masterminds—groups of like-minded people with a common mission—have been the single most important element of my growth. So, now I host a growing money mastermind network that is all about teaching and supporting others along their journey towards massive wealth. Find more information at MakeMoneyLiveWealthy.com/mastermind.

Mindset

Everything I talk about is ultimately related to one thing—your mindset. Of the ten steps in this book, the mindset is the most important on your journey towards wealth. As a result, this is the focus of my training. At MakeMoneyLiveWealthy.com/mindset, you'll find more information about how to build an unstoppable millionaire mindset.

Money

Money in and of itself isn't the only goal, but it sure does make everything else much easier. As a result, this is the other critical piece to which everything I talk about is related. It is my belief that if you take care of your financial situation and your mindset, everything else in life can much more easily fall into place. So take control of your financial future—learn those basic habits and practices and build that foundation on which you can build your dreams. I will help you through this process piece by piece.

The results of doing these things are everything that you *really* want—money, freedom, confidence, peace of mind, happiness, etc. I've been fortunate enough to achieve these things early on, and my hope is that this book, these steps, and these experts' advice will motivate you to move quickly towards

Appendix

your dreams. Just know that you can achieve anything you set your mind to. Make the decision and commit, and get on your path to wealth.

In closing, I want to say how appreciative I am that you have read this book. I receive messages from people every single day from all over the world, and it never fails to make my day. I love to hear about your victories and about the positive changes in your life. Keep taking massive action and always live wealthy.

Sincerely, thank you.

- Austin

The Experts

I have to give a huge thanks to the many experts interviewed on the YoPro Wealth podcast. Without them, this book of course would not have been created. Not only have I been impressed by their stories and successes, but they are each extremely genuine and selfless, as well. I can't thank them enough for their support, and strongly suggest that you check out their links and resources. Go to MakeMoneyLiveWealthy.com/podcastlist to see the complete list of interviews and experts.

Ann Wilson, self-made multi-millionaire, bestselling author of The Wealth Chef, TheWealthChef.com

Dan Miller, owner of 48 Days, LLC, bestselling author of 48 Days to the Work You Love, 48Days.com

Jack Schwager, iconic investing author of the Market Wizards series, JackSchwager.com

Richard Wilson, founder of the Billionaire Family Office and other businesses under the Wilson Holding Company, author, FamilyOfficesGroup.com

John Murphy, executive coach, founder of John Murphy International, JohnMurphyInternational.com

Todd Tresidder, former investment hedge fund manager, current financial coach and author, FinancialMentor.com

Ryan Holiday, award–winning author of Trust Me, I'm Lying and The Obstacle is the Way, RyanHoliday.net

Steve Burns, stock and options trader, author of the New Trader, Rich Trader series, NewTraderU.com

Larry Stevens, entrepreneur, founder of Opus Workspace, OpusWorkspace.com

Appendix

Chris Locurto, leadership and business coach, speaker, entrepreneur, ChrisLocurto.com

Michael Kawula - Michael Kawula, Bestselling Author of Connect, Serial Entrepreneur, Founder of SelfEmployedKing.com

Tom Basso, iconic investor spotlighted in Jack Schwager's Market Wizards series, Founder of Trendstat Capital Management

Justin Williams, successful real estate investor and entrepreneur, and host of HouseFlippingHQ.com blog and podcast

Josh Brown, entrepreneur, franchise attorney, and founder of The Law Office of Josh F. Brown, IndyFranchiseLaw.com

Patrick Schulte, investor, traveler, co-author of Live on the Margin, bumfuzzle.com

J. Massey, real estate investor, entrepreneur, author, and host of Cash Flow Diary podcast, CashFlowDiary.com

JV Crum III, CEO / Founder ConsciousMillionaire.com, Bestselling Author of Conscious Millionaire

David Wood, author, trainer, life coach, humanitarian and business leader, host of TheKickassLife.com podcast

Matt McWilliams author, Founder of Matt McWilliams Consulting, Inc., MattMcWilliams.com

Steve Stewart, debt expert, financial wellness coach, host of MoneyPlanSOS.com blog and podcast

Peter Voogd, serial entrepreneur, trainer, and Founder & CEO of RealVIPSuccess, RealVIPSuccess.com

Jason Vitug, CEO & co-founder of Phroogal.com

Matt Shoup, entrepreneur, author, and business coach, MattShoup.com

Hal Elrod, keynote speaker, coach, and bestselling author of The Miracle Morning, HalElrod.com

Taylor White, international real estate investor and coach, InternationalRealEstateListings.com

Jon Gordon, bestselling author of numerous books including The Energy Bus and The Carpenter, JonGordon.com

Mark Sieverkropp, author of Project: Success and co-host of Happen to Your Career podcast, Sieverkropp.com

Hugh Kimura, foreign exchange trader, founder of TradingHeroes.com

Mike Faith, Founder & CEO of Headsets.com, MikeFaith.com

Russell Wild, investment advisor, Principal at Global Portfolios, author of numerous books including Index Investing for Dummies, RussellWild.com

Philip Taylor, CPA, personal finance expert, PTMoney.com

Laurie Itkin, financial advisor, author of Every Woman Should Know Her Options, TheOptionsLady.com

Jim Wang, serial entrepreneur and finance expert, Founder of Bargaineering.com, MicroBlogger.com

Mike Michalowicz, entrepreneur and bestselling author of The Toilet Paper Entrepreneur and Profit First, MikeMichalowicz.com

Nick Loper, author, Owner of Bryck Media, Founder of SideHustleNation.com blog and podcast

Erlend Bakke, bestselling author of Never Work Again, speaker, CEO / Founder of YouSpin, ErlendBakke.com

Erez Katz, serial entrepreneur, co-founder and CEO of Lucena Research, LucenaResearch.com

Appendix

Kevin Johnson, serial entrepreneur, President of Johnson Media Inc., author of The Entrepreneur Mind, TheEntrepreneurMind.com

Coach Mike Basevic, behavioral strategist and performance coach, author, Founder of NoLimitsMentalEdge.com

Marcus Sheridan, entrepreneur and speaker, content marketing expert, TheSalesLion.com

Rob Wilson, engineer, entrepreneur and financial advisor, host of Movers & Shakers podcast, RobWilson.tv

Barrett Brooks, Director of Member Success for Fizzle.co, speaker and coach

Anton Ivanov, self-made millionaire, money coach, Founder of Financessful.com

Jonathan Duong, Chartered Financial Analyst, Certified Financial Planner, Founder and President of Wealth Engineers, WealthEngineersLLC.com

Jared Easley, entrepreneur and coach, host of StarveTheDoubts.com blog and podcast

Michael Kitces, Certified Financial Planner, speaker, Kitces.com

Pat Flynn, online business expert and entrepreneur, author of Let Go, SmartPassiveIncome.com

David Weliver, personal finance expert, founding editor of MoneyUnder30.com

Linda P. Jones, America's Wealth Mentor, finance coach, CEO of Be Wealthy & Smart, LindaPJones.com

Leisa Peterson, Certified Financial Planner, money mindfulness expert and Founder of WealthClinic, WealthClinic.com

Sean Ogle, online business coach, Founder of Location180.com

Make Money, Live Wealthy

Robert Farrington, Founder of TheCollegeInvestor.com and BeatThe9to5.com

Kate Northrup, author of Money: A Love Story, wellness entrepreneur, KateNorthrup.com

J. Money, blogger, hustler, founder of BudgetsAreSexy.com

Scott Barlow, career expert, co-host of HappenToYourCareer.com blog and podcast

Neil Patel, serial entrepreneur, founder of KISSmetrics, QuickSprout.com

Ruben Rojas, financial coach, entrepreneur and athlete, RubenRojas.com

John Lee Dumas, entrepreneur, Founder and host of EntrepreneurOnFire.com blog and podcast

Brittney Castro, Certified Financial Planner, founder of FinanciallyWiseWomen.com

Patrick Bet-David, serial entrepreneur and author of Doing the Impossible, CEO & Co-Founder of PHP Agency, PatrickBetDavid.com

August Turak, successful entrepreneur and award-winning author of Business Secrets of the Trappist Monks, AugustTurak.com

Trevor Blake, successful entrepreneur, New York Times bestselling author of Three Simple Steps, TrevorGBlake.com

Mindy Crary, financial coach, Certified Financial Planner, founder of CreativeMoney.biz

Billy Murphy, former professional poker player, serial entrepreneur, founder of Blue Fire Poker, ForeverJobless.com blog and podcast

Rob Berger, attorney, finance expert, founder of DoughRoller.net

Richard Weissman, professional trader, author of Trade Like a Casino, WeissmanSignals.com

Appendix

Kathleen Kingsbury, wealth psychology expert, author of How to Give Financial Advice to Couples, speaker, KBKWealthConnection.com

Ryan Michler, financial and investment advisor, Founder of Cittica Financial, host of Wealth Anatomy podcast, Cittica.com

Dr. Dennis Cummins, bestselling author of Turning Terrible into Terrific, expert trainer, DennisCummins.com

JD Roth, Founder of GetRichSlowly.org, author of Your Money: The Missing Manual

<u>Acknowledgements</u>

There were dozens of people that made this book a much easier process than I could have ever imagined.

Thanks for the constant feedback and guidance by my launch team and close network. You guys are rockstars and always go out of your way to help someone with seemingly never-ending questions.

For all of the great resources that I used to make this book a success, go to MakeMoneyLiveWealthy.com/bestseller-resources. To my editors, Mason Smith and Lori Draft, thank you for making a bad writer much better. To my cover designer, Zoran, thanks for the thousands of edits and tests. To Phil Serzo and Joe Shaffer, thanks for stepping up to lead the launch team. Peter Arnott, you've been a great experienced resource to help me get to #1–thank you. Timothy, Pasco, Uli, Sean, JV, Erica, Mark, Ryan, Tracey, Timur, Trevor, and many more–I am forever grateful for your honest and kind feedback and support. Mike, Kathleen, JD, Laurie, Erlend, Richard, and all of the other bestselling authors I talked to–I really appreciate all of your advice; thanks for paving the way for me!

And most importantly, to my family and friends that let me travel and work with ease and joy over the last few months–I owe you big time. Your support and excitement about the book made me even more eager to send it out into the world. For everything, I thank you.

Appendix

Resources

There are many free videos and resources that accompany this book to help teach you exactly what to do for each step. Sign up for free VIP membership at MakeMoneyLiveWealthy.com/bookguide.

Also, be sure to check out the YoPro Wealth podcast in iTunes or Stitcher. Visit YoProWealth.com for more details.

About the Author

Austin Netzley is a former athlete turned engineer, investor, entrepreneur and now author. He is the founder of ONE Pursuit Investments, as well as the host of the YoPro Wealth blog & podcast.

Austin overcame $80,000 of debt and a middle class mindset to find financial freedom early on. At the age of 27, Austin retired from corporate America to travel the world and scale his stock trading business while also doing what he is most passionate about: helping others take their money and their mindset to the next level.

For more information, please visit:
- AustinNetzley.com
- MakeMoneyLiveWealthy.com
- YoProWealth.com

Made in the USA
Lexington, KY
29 November 2014